INTRADAILY EXCHANGE RATE MOVEMENTS

Intradaily Exchange Rate Movements

by

Dominique M. Guillaume

*Catholic University of Louvain, Belgium and
Oxford University, United Kingdom*

KLUWER ACADEMIC PUBLISHERS
BOSTON / DORDRECHT / LONDON

A C.I.P. Catalogue record for this book is available from the Library of Congress.

ISBN 0-7923-8696-5

Published by Kluwer Academic Publishers,
P.O. Box 17, 3300 AA Dordrecht, The Netherlands.

Sold and distributed in North, Central and South America
by Kluwer Academic Publishers,
101 Philip Drive, Norwell, MA 02061, U.S.A.

In all other countries, sold and distributed
by Kluwer Academic Publishers,
P.O. Box 322, 3300 AH Dordrecht, The Netherlands.

Printed on acid-free paper

Printed in the Netherlands.

Contents

Preface

In recent years, a broad consensus has emerged among economists that the different vintages of macro-economic models have largely failed to account for the foreign exchange rates movements in the short to medium run, that is, from daily up to quarterly or even yearly frequencies (see e.g. Frankel and Rose (1995) for a recent survey). Only in the very long run do these models appear to have a predictive power superior to a random-walk, which is the simplest benchmark one could consider (Mark, 1995).

Therefore, rather than to try linking foreign exchange rates with fundamentals, another route pursued by researchers was to question the rational expectation hypothesis assumed in these models. Using surveys amongst traders, they brought to light the heterogeneity of their expectations (e.g., Takagi, 1991). More important even, it seems that traders have different expectations depending on the time horizon at which they are looking. In the short run, expectations tend to be destabilising whereas in the long run they are regressive towards a long run fundamental equilibrium. This is quite understandable as it also appeared that traders' preferred category of models in the short run is technical analysis, a broad class of techniques that extrapolate the information contained in past prices (Frankel and Froot, 1990; Allen and Taylor, 1992). The use of technical analysis as a systematic explanation of the behaviour of exchange rates movements is, however, still a matter of debate because it would imply the existence of unexploited arbitrage opportunities. On the other hand, it has gained some academic acceptability since it was rationalised in theoretical models combining fundamentals and extrapolative expectations (De Long et al., 1990; De Grauwe and Dewachter, 1993). Some simulation studies have also demonstrated the potential profitability of technical analysis (Levich and Thomas, 1992).

Another route followed by researchers was to investigate the statistical process of foreign exchange rate returns. Indeed, foreign exchange rate returns do not have to be identically and independently distributed as in a random walk to follow a martingale process. Dependencies could come through the second moment or even higher moments without implying predictability of the mean. As a matter of fact, already in the 60's, Mandelbrot (1963) had shown that periods of quiescence tend to be followed by periods of quiescence rather than periods of turbulence and vice-versa. This clustering of the volatility process was first made endogenous in the Auto-Regressive Conditional Heteroskedastic process (ARCH) by Engle (1982) and its generalised version by Bollerslev (1986). The ARCH model has now expanded into a whole family of models (Bollerslev et al., 1992) as further properties of the volatility process, such as its long run memory, were unveiled. Though, an economic explanation for the clustering of volatility is yet to be given.

Debate also arose on whether the statistical process underlying the distribution of foreign exchange rates returns was more akin to, for instance, the ARCH process, a Student-T or a Cauchy distribution. These developments are especially important if one considers foreign exchange rate returns from a portfolio optimisation perspective where the first two moments are the central parameters of interest, the mean representing the average return and the variance the risk involved.

The next natural step to broaden the understanding of foreign exchange markets was to look at intradaily foreign exchange movements since more than 70% of the 1.4 billion USD average foreign exchange daily trading volume takes place between traders who close their position at the end of the day (B.I.S., 1993). However, it was not before the very end of the eighties that research on the intradaily exchange rates was begun, mainly due to technical obstacles. These obstacles are quite formidable and range from the actual purchase of the data from data vendors such as Reuters and their massive storage on computers, to the transformation and filtering of the data into clean time series that can be used. Fortunately, very much at the same time as Goodhart (1989) published the first paper using a series of two weeks of intradaily foreign exchange rates , Olsen & Associates, a Swiss private research institute,

had made the necessary technological, human, and indeed capital investment required for a more systematic collection of this data. When the
work contained in this book was started in 1993, it benefited from the
enormous generosity of Olsen & Associates who shared their data which
by then covered a period of seven years, that is, a couple of millions of
data points. An extensive study of this data set has resulted in the different chapters of this book, some of which were written in collaboration
with the Olsen & Associates research team.

The research covered in this book has two main purposes: the systematic study of the characteristics of intradaily data and an empirical
investigation using intradaily data of the three approaches to the modelling of foreign exchange rates outlined above.

In an introductory chapter, a more systematic attempt to classify
the successive waves of foreign exchange rate models is proposed using
a typology based on the type of asymptotic equilibria.

The first objective of the book is then addressed to in the second
chapter which surveys the main stylised facts on the intradaily foreign
exchange rates . These facts provide a partial answer to some of the
questions raised above. For example, thanks to the extremely large
number of data available a study of the tails of the distribution could
help categorise the distribution of exchange rates returns without falling
into the non-negligible small sample bias usually associated with such
studies. The nature of the volatility clustering captured by the Auto-
Regressive Conditional Heteroskedastic family of models could partly be
understood in terms of the interaction between different markets. The
relevance of macro-economic modelling could be tested in a nonlinear
dynamic framework which does not imply predictability per se. And, the
very short-lived impact of macro-economic news announcements could
be verified.

The analysis of this extremely large data set of intradaily foreign exchange rates has also uncovered new regularities of the foreign exchange
rates. For example, parameters could not be disaggregated from daily
frequency estimates into intradaily estimates as predicted theoretically

for a homogenous GARCH process, a hint at the presence of a different expectation process at the intradaily frequency than, say, at the daily or even monthly frequencies. On the other hand, intradaily data revealed the existence of a fractal law that links the average absolute foreign exchange price changes measured at different frequencies to these frequencies in a very different way from the Gaussian, Student-T, Cauchy or GARCH distributions. The seemingly random large changes of the persistence parameters of the volatility in the Auto- Regressive Conditional Heteroskedastic model over relatively long periods is consistent with important structural breaks which are yet to be explained in terms of changes of the underlying fundamentals, institutions, policy decision rules or contagion effects.

Another important issue is the price formation process that takes place every other couple of seconds or minutes, also termed 'market microstructure ' as first coined by Garman (1976). Whereas there is a huge theoretical and empirical literature on the topic for stock markets (see, for example, (O'Haara, 1995), progress in the understanding of the price formation process of the foreign exchange markets has been limited partly due to institutional differences from stock markets and partly due to data limitations. For instance, foreign exchange markets differ from most of stock exchange markets in that they are decentralised rather than centralised markets which prevents the easy transposition of stock markets models. Another difference from stock markets is that foreign exchange markets are virtually continuously open around the world. As a consequence, whereas stock market micro- structure explanations for the widening of the bid-ask spread at the end of the trading day may be valid for one particular market, say Europe, they cannot account at the same time for the absence of widening of this bid-ask spread in another simultaneously opened market, say New York (see, for example, Hsieh and Kleidon, 1996).

In common with most other studies, our data set has important shortcomings for tests of microstructure hypotheses in that it is constituted of indicative quotes rather than transaction prices (which overestimate spreads at frequencies higher than 10 to 15 minutes by a factor of 3) and that it does not include information on the traded volume. Recent work using a two weeks data set of a large trader's transaction data, has been able to avoid such short-comings, providing important insights into the microstructure of the foreign exchange market. In a series of papers recently brought in a book , (Lyons, 1996b; Lyons, 1995; Lyons, 1996a; Lyons, 1997; Lyons, 1999) shows that both the asymmetric information and the inventory channels seem to play a role in explaining the price formation process in the foreign exchange markets (contrary to findings for the stock market, e.g. Madhavan and Smith (1991)).

The second objective of this book is to investigate empirically the three different approaches to the modelling of foreign exchange rates mentioned earlier using intradaily data. In the third chapter, the macroeconomic or fundamental approach to the foreign exchange rates was tested in a very general way. Our test is based on deterministic tests developed in chaos theory but extends them in that it includes the possibility of a small stochastic component, a feature more in line with economic intuition. This approach is independent both of the particular functional form of a model and of the choice of a set of relevant fundamentals. Furthermore, the dynamic specification of such test is richer than most previous tests as it does not imply predictability of the process. Thus, rather than accepting (or rejecting) a specific macroeconomic model, we are able to accept (or reject) the fact that the dynamics of foreign exchange rates can be determined by a small set of fundamentals.

The univariate time series approach to the foreign exchange markets is illustrated in the next two chapters: chapter 5 uses the now common Generalised Auto-Regressive Conditional Heteroskedastic (GARCH) process, whereas chapter 4 adopts a time deformation framework, a technique which allows one to reflect the subjective notion of time held by traders. Four important issues are dealt with in these chapters. First, we show the importance of the geographical dispersion of traders around the world for the estimation of these models and propose a solution to avoid the mis- specifications it introduces. Second, we show that the parameters of the process do not aggregate from one frequency to another as predicted theoretically, pointing out the presence of distinct news arrival processes at different frequencies. Third, we uncover important structural changes of the parameters of the processes from one sub-sample period to another. Four, we disentangle several sources of nonlinearities in intradaily exchange rates.

The technical analysis approach is investigated in chapter 6 where some earlier results on the profitability of such techniques are checked in a relatively simple framework. The three main differences with previous work in the area are the use of data at intra- daily frequencies where such techniques are generally supposed to be used by traders; the use of trading ranges coming from intradaily Reuters' surveys among traders in addition to trading ranges computed from simulations; and the incorporation of transaction costs. In an area where the literature remains controversial, the findings of the absence profitability of these rules for our intradaily data set will hopefully trigger further enquiries into the usefulness of chartism.

The above four chapters do by no means provide a definitive answer on the relative suitability of the respective modelling approaches; rather, they are intended to show how these approaches can be used in the context of intradaily foreign exchange rate movements and to highlight some of the pitfalls inherent to such exercise.

Acknowledgements and Copyrights

Chapter 2 originally appeared as "From the bird's eye to the microscope: A survey of new stylized facts of the intra-daily foreign exchange markets" by Dominique Guillaume, Michel Dacorogna, Rakhal Davé, Ulrich Müller, Richard Olsen and Olivier Pictet in Finance and Stochastics, vol. 1 (1997), pp. 95-129.

A previous version of Chapter 3 appeared as "A Low-Dimensional Fractal Attractor in the Foreign Exchange Markets?" in R. Trippi (ed.), Chaos and Nonlinear Dynamics in the Financial Markets, Irwin Publ., (1995), pp. 269-294.

Chapter 4 was circulated as an Olsen& Associates working paper entitled "Unveiling Nonlinearities through Time Scales transformations" by Dominique Guillaume, Olivier Pictet, Ulrich Müller and Michel Dacorogna.

Chapter 5 was circulated as an Olsen& Associates working paper entitled "On the intra-daily performance of GARCH processes" by Dominique Guillaume, Michel Dacorogna and Olivier Pictet.

Chapter 6 appeared as "Do Technical Trading Rules Generate Profits? Conclusions from the Intra-Day Foreign Exchange Market" by Riccardo Curcio, Charles Goodhart, Dominique Guillaume and Richard Payne in International Journal of Finance and Economics, vol. 2 (1997), pp. 267-280.

I am most grateful and indeed indebted to Filip Abraham, Tim Bollerslev, Michel Dacorogna, Paul De Grauwe, Charles Goodhart, Richard Payne, Olivier Pictet and Casper de Vries for numerous discussions and comments. Collaborating with some of them has been a great pleasure. The Olsen&Associates team provided a generous hospitality at a crucial time for some of the work presented in this book. The Belgian National Scientific Foundation and the Human Capital Mobility Program of the European Union supported financially the work.

Chapter 1

A Typology of Foreign Exchange Rates Models

In this introductory chapter, we propose a typology of foreign exchange models according to their asymptotic equilibria. This typology is, of course, only indicative and does not cover all the different types of foreign exchange models. In particular, models based on the use of technical analysis such as in the last chapter do not fit very well in that typology, nor do models based on the microstructure of the markets (see Lyons, 1999). Nonetheless, the following figure should give a good overview of the different approaches adopted in this book.

The following mathematical definitions and examples should clarify the above figure.

Define the phase space X as R^m or infinite dimensional and the function $f : X \to X$ as continuous, and continuously differentiable as many times as necessary and denote f^t denotes the tth iteration of the function f ($t \in N$).

Define the orbit of a point x in X as the set $\{x, f(x), f^2(x), ...\}$.

Define A as an attracting set; that is, A is a compact set $\subset X$ with open neighbourhood U such that

(i) $\forall$ open set $V \subset A$, we have $f^t(U) \subset V$ for $t \to \infty$;

(ii) $f^t(A) = A, \forall t$;

(iii) $\cup_{t>0}(f^t)^{-1}(U) = X$. Property (iii) says the basin of attraction of

1

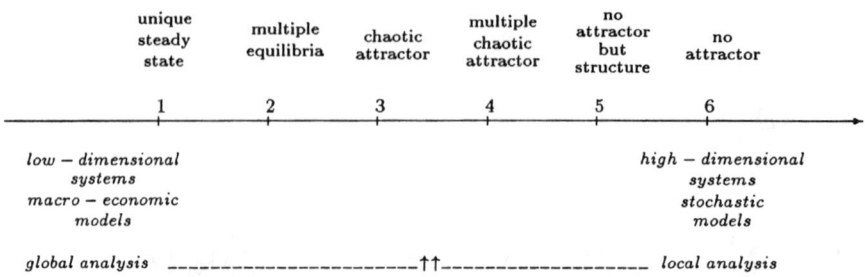

Figure 1.1: A typology of asymptotic equilibria for foreign exchange models
The different potential types of equilibria are classified according to their
complexity. Going to the right, the equilibrium gets more and more complex. The number of degrees of freedom or dimension of the attractor
also increases as one goes from the left to the right on the figure. The
fourth type of equilibrium is at the limit between low-dimensional macro-
economic models and infinite dimensional stochastic models. Note that,
although of great interest for our exposition, the two last types of equilibria do not possess an attractor.

A is the whole phase space X.

Define an attractor as an attracting set A, for which there exists an
initial value $x_0 \in A$, such that the orbit of x_0 is dense in A (that is all
experimental points $f^t(x)$ accumulates on A for large t). In practice, x_0
has some (unknown) probability distribution on X.

Then, we can define the following types of asymptotic equilibria or
attractors:

1. **A unique steady state or attractive fixed point**:

   $A = \{x^*\}$.

example: $f(x) = \mu x(1 - x)$ for $1 < \mu < 3$ and $x_0 \in]0, 1[$ (the Feigenbaum attractor)

2. **Multiple equilibria:**

$A = \{x^{i*}, i = 1, ..., n\}$, and $f^t(x^i) = x^{i*}$ for $t \to \infty$ depending on the initial conditions x^i.

A special case of multiple equilibria is the periodic steady state where $f^t(x^*) = x^*$ but $f^T(x^*) \neq x^*$, $0 < T < t$.

example: $f(x) = \mu x(1 - x)$ for $\mu = 3.3$ and $x_0 \in]0, 1[$ (the Feigenbaum attractor)

3. **Chaotic attractor:**

$A \subset X$, and $f^t(x^i) = x^{i*}$, $x^{i*} \in A$ for $t \to \infty$ depending on the initial conditions x^i and

$$lim \ sup|f^n(x) - f^n(y)| \geq \varepsilon$$
$$lim \ inf|f^n(x) - f^n(y)| = 0$$

for some $\varepsilon > 0$, and $\forall \ x, y \in A$, with $x \neq y$. That is, nearby trajectories on this set always eventually wander apart but all trajectories also always eventually pass arbitrarily close to one another. This means both that small differences in initial conditions eventually mean completely different paths, and that knowing the initial conditions is of little help in forecasting the state of the system in the sufficiently distant future.

example: $f(x, y) = (1 - ax^2 + y, bx)$, with $a = 1.4$, $b = 0.3$ and $(x_0, y_0) = (0.001, 0)$ (the Henon map)

4. **Multiple chaotic attractors:**

$A = \cup (A^j)(j = 1, ..., m)$ with $A \subseteq X$ and $A^j \subset X$, $f^t(x^{ji}) = x^{ji*}, x^{ji*} \in A^j$ for $t \to \infty$ depending on the initial conditions x^i and

$$lim\ sup|f^n(x) - f^n(y)| \geq \varepsilon$$
$$lim\ inf|f^n(x) - f^n(y)| = 0$$

for some $\varepsilon > 0$, and $\forall\ x, y \in A^j$, with $x \neq y$ and $\cap(A^i, A^j)$ $(i, j = 1, ..., m) \neq 0$ to satisfy the irreducibility property of an attractor (i.e., the union of two disjoint attractors is not considered an attractor).

The concept of a non-uniform attractor was introduced by Gallez and Babloyants (1991) in their analysis of the heart beats to account for the presence of two distinct though intersecting attractors in the phase space; that is, for certain initial conditions, the dynamic path can fall on either attractor. In the above definition, we extend this empirical concept to the case where there are many of these intersecting attractors and where their union (A) possibly represents the whole phase space; that is, formally, there is no global attractor.

5. **No attractor, but structure:**

$A = X$

Here again, we cannot speak of an attractor since the whole phase space represents the space of potential equilibria. But, contrary to the previous case, there is no dynamic equilibrium here. Though, by contrast to the next type of equilibrium, some structure may be observed in that phase space, through dependencies in the higher moments.

This is the case of so-called coloured noise process, where $x_t = g(\varepsilon_t)$, $\forall t$, g is continuous and continuously differentiable and ε_t is not i.i.d..

example: $x_t = \varepsilon = \eta_t \sqrt{h_t}$, where η_t is i.i.d. $N(0, 1)$ and
$h_t = \alpha_0 + \alpha_1 \varepsilon_{t-1}^2 + ... + \alpha_q \varepsilon_{t-q}^2$ (ARCH(q) process)

6. **No attractor:**

$A = X$

Here, the attractor is again the whole phase space, but, this time, there is no apparent structure whatsoever. This is the case of a white noise process:

$x_t = \varepsilon_t$, $\forall t$, and ε_t is i.i.d..

The above types of asymptotic equilibria can be viewed as particular cases of the following general model of the dynamics:
$x_t = f^t(x_0) + g(\varepsilon_t)$ where ε_t is not i.i.d..
In the first four cases, the dynamic path is mainly determined by the deterministic component ($f^t(x_0)$) whereas in the last two cases, the noise component ($g(\varepsilon_t)$) dominates.

1.1 Models with fixed point

These models are mostly macro-economic models of the asset market type usually with one representative agent and a few variables or "fundamentals" like real income, domestic and foreign supply of money, interest rate, price level, balance of international payments and expected value of the spot exchange rate in the next time period. These models are either partial equilibrium (linear) models like the monetary (Frenkel and Mussa, 1985) and portfolio balance models (Branson and Henderson, 1985) general equilibrium models à la Lucas with a cash-in-advance constraint (Obstfeld and Stockman, 1985) or overlapping generations (Kareken and Wallace, 1981).

The dynamics of these models only arise through exogenous shocks to the fundamentals. In absence of these shocks, prices fully discount the future path of the fundamentals through rational expectations. The current spot rate is the expected discounted sum of all future market fundamentals. Changes in the spot rate will result from "news"about future fundamentals. Thus, to the extent that changes in the economic fundamentals are predictable, changes in the spot exchange rate are predictable. In this framework, central bank interventions can affect the exchange rate only if they affect the fundamentals. However, shocks to the fundamentals do not need to be restricted to the monetary sphere. In the general equilibrium type of FX models, the explanation of movement of exchange rates is extended to the real sphere by allowing the exchange rate to play a role in accommodating preferences or productivity shocks.

These models are natural extensions of models developed for domestic economies and were quite appealing by the economic rationale they provide for the medium and long term evolution of FX rates. But unfortunately, with the exception of hyper-inflationary regimes[1], their empirical validation with monthly or quarterly data has been a failure:

1. fundamentals are indeed hard to predict and the structural parameters need to be estimated. Even in the best case where these models could provide an ex-post explanations of FX rates movements, the validity of this explanation was restricted to a sub-period (for example, the over-shooting model could explain the movements of the US/DEM in the period 1980-1985 but not afterwards). One explanation for this lack of a stable exchange rate equation is the Lucas (1976) critique which states that the parameters of current exchange rate models are not structural since they change with different policy regimes.

2. Even more central than the structural breaks in the parameters are changes in the relevant fundamentals. For example in the USA, the focus of the markets has shifted from real interest differentials

in the early 1980s to US budget and current account deficits from the mid-1980s to the present. The current account was also an important explanatory variable in the late 1970s. Unemployment was the focus in the beginning of the 1990s and who knows, environment might well be the focus in the year 2010s. Such changes in the underlying views on the fundamentals may explain why even in the very long run these models cannot explain deviations from the rationally expected path known as the forward premium puzzle (Engle and Hamilton, 1990) or the random behaviour of the real exchange rate (Levich, 1985)[2].

3. Finally, these models can neither explain the short term statistical properties of FX rates, nor the much higher volatility of FX rates relative to the fundamentals, although in the latter case one should note that the specification of the model allows FX rate to be even more volatile than their component fundamental factors[3].

It is therefore understandable that monetary policies based on these types of mechanisms proved to be quite ineffective, notwithstanding the problem of their credibility (see, for example, Weber, 1995). An additional reason for the inefficiency of central bank interventions is the relatively small share of their total exchange reserves with respect to the daily turnover of FX market[4]. The direct impact of actual central banks interventions on the exchange rate is therefore quite limited. Perhaps more important, such interventions could signal a change in the expectations of future central bank policy, which has a potentially quite large indirect effect. However, as we shall see below, the expectation mechanisms of FX market participants can result in a quite complex dynamics whose effects are difficult to predict.

With the dismal performance of the above category of models, economists have been thinking of several alternatives. These alternatives involve that:

1. Exogenous shocks are not necessarily restricted to a few fundamentals but can involve any type of news;

2. The relationships between the variables need not to be linear and can lead to much more complex types of equilibrium;

3. Deviations from the value predicted by the fundamentals can result from other possibly not rational or heterogeneous expectation mechanism.

Alternatives (2) and (3) are the basis for the models described in sections 1.3 to 1.5, whereas alternative (1) is central to the models proposed in the last two sections.

1.2   Models with multiple equilibria

There are several distinct although possibly complementary ways in which the case of multiple equilibria can arise from : (i) an indeterminacy due to the non-linear form of the function; (ii) the coexistence of several fundamental models; (iii) expectations rationally deviating from the fundamentals; (iv) heterogeneous, non rational expectations; (v) the learning mechanism of agents.

1. **Indeterminacy due to the non-linear form of the function.**

   This indeterminacy does not need to reflect inefficiency or irrationality. In the case of the partial equilibrium type of model, it can result from the direct introduction of nonlinearities like in the model of Chiarella (1990) who introduces a nonlinear demand function for foreign assets into the Dornbusch model.

   General equilibrium models on the other hand can also present indeterminacy of the equilibrium under certain conditions such as different values of the coefficient of risk aversion and market imperfections. Although much of the studies done in this area do not include the case of international currency markets, this is an important emerging literature initiated by the paper of Grandmont (1985) in the context of an overlapping generation model and Bewley (1986) for the case of an indefinitely-lived agent with a cash-in-advance constraint[5]. Using a Mundell-Fleming set-up, Chen (1992) uses the same line of reasoning as these papers by modifying the gross inter-temporal elasticity of substitution with respect to the expected change in the real exchange rate.

2. **The coexistence of several fundamental models.**

   A first approach developed by Hamilton (1988) is simply to allow for the presence of regime shifts within the same fundamentals framework by introducing a latent variable that signals the probability of a regime shift. The second more general approach is to also allow for the coexistence of several fundamentals or macro-economics models by introducing a more general encompassing model (Goldberg and Frydman, 1993).

3. **Expectations rationally deviating from the fundamentals.**

   There are at least three main ways in which expectations could rationally deviate from the fundamentals: temporary mimetic contagion (rational bubble), exogenous (stochastic) shocks to beliefs (sunspots) or statistical problems "peso" problem).

   Rational bubbles arise when market participants view the exchange rate as a (linear) function of not only fundamentals and but also of another variable that expresses the sentiment of the markets. Until it bursts of, this bubble component causes the exchange rate to reach another equilibrium than the fundamental equilibrium. Although appealing by their straightforward way of modelling beliefs, empirical tests of the existence of bubbles are usually unconvincing (Flood and Hodrick, 1990). Besides, the existence of rational bubbles implies that national and foreign portfolio should be imperfect substitutes, which does not go with the tendency to integrate financial markets.

   The second explanation for the deviation of rational expectations from their fundamental path rests on the existence of stochastic shocks to beliefs or *sunspots*. Sunspots differ from bubbles in that they (possibly) involve an infinity of equilibria corresponding to

the fundamental equilibrium or even the rational bubble equilibrium. Their existence is usually difficult to rule out theoretically[6].
For example, in the study of the Mundell-Fleming model by Chen
(1992) cited above, sunspots are shown to arise under certain conditions for the inter-temporal elasticity of substitution with respect
to the expected change in the real exchange rate. However, as of
yet, no empirical test of sunspots have been devised.

The third explanation lies in the so-called *peso problem* which char-
acterises statistical inference problem in an environment characterised by changes in policy regime or financial innovation. Peso
problems result when agents incorporate a small probability of an
unusual event (like a large devaluation of a currency or a change
in a country's exchange rate policy) in their expectations, but the
unusual event does not occur or occurs infrequently during the
sample period used for the analysis. Although the potential for
peso problems will remain until data samples contain enough of
these exceptional episodes, the probability that they are at the
origin of deviations from the fundamentals is quite low (Froot and
Thaler, 1990).

4. **Heterogeneous, non rational expectations.**

A potentially more fruitful explanation for the deviation of expectations from the fundamentals is the existence of heterogeneous,
non rational expectations[7] as evidenced by various studies on survey data on exchange rate expectations[8]. Typically, survey participants follow different models of expectation according to the
horizons at which they trade. In the short run, expectations tend
to be de-stabilising, that is to follow the trend. Survey forecast errors are usually found to be correlated with information available
to market participants so that survey participants could improve
their forecast accuracy by putting more weight on the current spot
rate and less on fundamental factors when predicting future spot
rates. On the other hand, in the long run expectations tend to
be regressive and to follow the fundamentals. The integration of

both types of expectations is the core of the model of DeGrauwe and Dewachter (1993) which shows the potential existence of multiple equilibria. Formal empirical testing of this type of models has however yet to be done.

5. **The learning mechanism of agents.**

   Even in the hypothesis of a unique asymptotic equilibrium, market participants could have to learn about the process leading to that equilibrium, so that many different temporary equilibria may be experienced (see Grandmont and Laroque (1986) for an early reference).

1.3   Models with chaotic attractors

Most of the mechanisms leading to the existence multiple equilibria can be at the origin of chaotic dynamics; that is, the nonlinear form of the function (Chiarella (1990) and Chen (1992), the coexistence of several fundamental models (Goldberf and Frydman, 1993), heterogeneous (non) rational expectations (DeGrauwe and Dewachter, 1993) and the learning mechanism of agents.

Chaotic dynamics is very appealing as it provides a (dynamic) generalisation of the two other types of low-dimensional systems[9]. Another feature of this type of equilibrium which is especially interesting in the case of FX rates, is the fact that it does not imply (global) predictability of the system (see Section 1), a well-known property of FX rates (Diebold and Nason, 1990).

The presence of such dynamics in theoretical models is usually derived by using the one-dimensional Li-Yorke (1975) framework. Higher dimensional tests are still based on simulations which require very large amounts of data. Unfortunately, the latter requirement is also valid for empirical tests of chaos which make earlier studies of the presence of chaos unreliable[10].

1.4   Models with multiple attractors

As we have seen in Figure   this category of equilibrium aims at filling
the gap between the low-dimensional and the infinite-dimensional types
of models. As mathematical tools have not yet been developed to test
the existence of this type of equilibrium, this category is therefore only
tentative. Needless to say then, that no economic models that would fit
into this category have yet been developed.

One such a model could be briefly described as follows: in the long
run, FX rates would switch from one attractor to the other as a result of
the (more or less) random role played by the underlying fundamentals,
whereas in the short to medium run, they would wander around the
attractor in a (globally) unpredictable way as a result of the trend-
following behaviour of market participants at these horizons.

1.5   Models with no attractor

The hypothesis that FX prices follow a random walk with the FX returns being a white noise process was first made by Bachelier in 1900.
More recently, Meese and Rogoff (1983) used it as the simplest linear
benchmark model to reject the first category of macro-economic models
outlined above. It is as of yet the most simple alternative to structural
models. In this approach, prices are globally unpredictable as they incorporate immediately any relevant news. Markets are thus efficient in
the meaning of Fama (1965) as no insider information is available at
least on broad markets such as the DEM or the YEN against the USD.
In the absence of structural models policy makers cannot affect the markets in whatever direction. Market participants on the other hand are
left with the optimisation of their portfolio by a risk - return approach
of the markets based on the normal distribution of the random walk.

While this model indeed fitted the statistical properties of weekly
or monthly data, at higher frequencies, a richer structure of the second
moment has been unveiled that makes this approach inadequate. In
particular, the risk - return maximising framework underestimates the

risk and ignores the structure of the markets. This is well-known to practitioners in option markets where the definition of the volatility is often the most crucial assumption in the models.

1.6 Models with no attractor but involving some structure

With the availability of daily data, the presence of nonlinear structures in FX returns due to the short and long term auto-correlation (memory) of the volatility (Engle, 1982) and the fatness of their tails (Westerfield, 1977) became very apparent. This motivated the development of two broad classes of nonlinear statistical models.

The first approach was the development of more sophisticated statistical process such as the discrete Auto Regressive Conditionally Heteroskedastic (ARCH) model (Engle, 1982). Successive generations of the ARCH models tried to capture more and more of the structure of FX rate as the latter was being unveiled. The explanation given to make this approach still consistent with the efficient market hypothesis is the presence of heterogeneous agents between which there might be spillovers of information from one category to the other. Such models include geographically heterogeneous agents (Engle et al., 1990), the presence of central banks (Hsieh, 1992) and agents with different information sets (Chauveau and Topol, 1993).

The second approach starts from the fact that market participants might have a subjective notion of time different from the physical time framework in which changes to the fundamentals take place. This approach was first originated by Clark (1973) and Allais (1974). More recently, Stock (1988) developed a model of time deformation where exchange rates could exhibit a stationary linear relation to fundamentals when viewed in the appropriate time scale. Indeed, in this model, time speeds up when an unusually large amount of economic news must be processed by the market.

Footnotes

(1) De Grauwe et al. (1985) shows the bad performance of these models even in the case of hyper-inflationary regimes like the German hyper-inflation between the two World Wars.

(2) See the survey of Froot and Thaler (1990) for a discussion.

(3) The variance of the spot rate can be higher than the variance of the fundamentals if the covariance's between fundamental factors are such that their variances combine to push the variance of the spot rate still higher.

(4) Note that if central banks fully cooperate and make a credible commitment towards sustaining the FX rate, they will be able to create any amount of money necessary in order to defend the FX rate.

(5) See the survey of Boldrin and Woodford (1990).

(6) See the survey of Guesnerie and Woodford (1992).

(7) Here, expectations are said to be non rational in that market participants do not incorporate all the available information in their models of the exchange rate.

(8) See the survey of Takagi (1991).

(9) Models exhibiting chaotic dynamics usually also possess a unique steady state or multiple equilibria, depending on the values taken by the parameters of the model.

(10) See chapter 3 for more details on the conditions of reliability of chaos tests.

Chapter 2

From the Bird's Eye to the Microscope: A Survey of New Stylised Facts

2.1 Introduction

Since the beginning of the 1990s, academic researchers have been gaining new insights into the behaviour of the foreign exchange (FX) markets through analysing intradaily data. Indeed, much information about the FX markets, both quantitative and qualitative, was not used up to now. Daily data which were much used in the 80's, represent only a very small subset of the information available at intradaily frequencies as they really are only the average of five intradaily quoted prices of the largest banks around a particular time. The number of data points available intradaily is 100 to 1000 times larger. Furthermore, the actual news or information at the disposal of the traders with the corresponding time stamp is displayed along with FX rates quotations on the data vendors screens. Finally, in addition to the volatility and the spread, new quantities for the description of the price evolution like the tick frequency or the directional change frequency can also be directly computed from the more comprehensive data set.

On the basis of this information set, there is now a rapidly growing body of empirical studies on the behaviour of the intradaily FX markets. This is especially interesting in that it opens new paths for understanding the behaviour of financial markets and suggests the widening of concepts such as risk or market efficiency. The analysis of intradaily data may also help clarify the different behaviour of intra-day traders, whose operations account for more than 75 % (Bank of International Settlements, 1996) of the FX market volume. Finally, as we shall see in more details in the following chapters, this set of facts on the intradaily FX rates sheds some new light on different modelling approaches to the FX market.

This chapter also offers some innovative ideas[1]. First, it proposes definitions of the variables to be studied and points out their limitations. Second, we distinguish between the general characteristics of intradaily data and those of the process of price formation that takes place at the highest frequency (within the 10 to 15 minutes time-interval) in order to highlight the specificity of this process. Third, different major issues such as the characterisation of the distribution of the price change, the definition and the use of the time-scale, the concept of risk or market efficiency, the process of learning and the modelling approaches to the market will be tackled throughout the survey.

Our focus is on the nominal spot exchange rates of major currencies. In particular we do not study well-known relationships between spot rates and other financial variables such as forward rates or interest rates which have not yet been investigated with intradaily data. Experience has indeed shown that known and well accepted empirical regularities of daily or weekly data do not always hold up in intradaily analysis. Moreover, the different structures of these financial markets may play an important role for the analysis of their statistical properties. We have also not systematically investigated the relationship between exchange rates and major macro-economic variables although new insights on the way to tackle this issue are presented.

As will be shown, looking at intradaily data, the homogeneity of market agents apparent at lower, weekly of daily, frequencies disappears. A new wealth of structure is uncovered that demonstrates the complexity of the FX market. This complexity can be explained by the interaction of market agents with heterogeneous objectives resulting from their different geographical location, the various types of their institutional constraints and their risk profiles. This is the key for future modelling of the dynamics of the markets.

The remainder of this chapter is organised as follows. Section 2.2 briefly describes the functioning of the foreign exchange markets and the data. Section 2.3 proposes a set of definitions for the variables under study. Section 2.4 regroups the set of empirical regularities under three different topics: the distribution aspects of the price process, the process of price formation and the heterogeneous structure of the markets. Section 2.5 concludes the chapter.

2.2 Description of the Foreign Exchange Market

The usual description of the FX markets made by international organisations such as the Bank for International Settlement or the International Monetary Fund emphasises the presence of different geographical markets and different types of agents (Bank for International Settlements, 1993; International Monetary Fund, 1993). However, this essential fact was not very apparent from the inspection of daily or weekly data and its implications were seldom considered in theoretical modelling. In this section, we shall summarise the essential descriptive knowledge we have of the FX market. Additionally, we describe the main source and type of data available for this market. As we shall see, the information content of intradaily data is much richer than that of daily or weekly data. However, the extend to which this information set can be increased and the degree of precision one can obtain are limited. This is reflected in the distinct characteristics of extremely high frequency data corresponding to the price formation process.

The FX market is a 24 hours global market, mostly inactive during weekends and during national holidays. The first observation of the week arrives at 22:30 Greenwich Mean Time (GMT) on Sunday with the opening of the Asian markets and the last observation comes from the West Coast of the USA at about 22:30 (GMT) on Friday[2]. Although the FX market is virtually global through its electronic linkages, its activity pattern can be divided into three continental components: East Asia with Tokyo as major trading center, Europe with London as major trading center and America with New York as major trading center[3] (Goodhart and Demos, 1990). Except for the four major currencies against the USD (DEM, JPY, GBP and CHF)[4] currencies tend to be traded more specifically in their own geographical markets. As we shall see in Section 2.4 below, both these global and local characteristics of the FX markets are reflected in the statistical properties of the data.

The FX market is also the largest financial market with a daily turnover[5] of USD 832 billion in April 1992 (Bank for International Settlements, 1993): that is, more than the total non-gold reserves (USD 555.6 billion) of all industrial countries in 1992 (International Monetary Fund, 1993) and more than the triple of the turnover in 1986. This fast growing volume of transactions is increasingly made up of short term, intradaily, transactions and results from the interaction of traders with different time-horizons, risk-profiles or regulatory constraints. On the one side, the non-financial institutions such as non-financial corporations, institutional investors (mutual funds, pension funds, insurance companies) and hedge funds[6] are shifting their FX activities from long term (buy and hold) investment to short term (profit-making) transactions. This movement is both enabled and enhanced by the development of real-time information systems and the decrease of transaction costs following the liberalisation of cross-border financial flows. On the other side, this flow of short and long term transactions initiated by non-financial institutions on the retail market is the origin of an even larger − by a factor of four to five times − flow of intradaily transactions between the dealers (the 50 largest banks and a few securities houses) on the wholesale market.

These dealers who are not usually allowed to take overnight positions, move to reduce their risk with each other (Lyons, 1996a). Still on the wholesale market, but in contrast with other players, central banks can afford relatively large open positions and can thereby have a significant impact on the market in the long run. These different types of traders can of course be found within the same company or the same type of institution[7]. Again, their presence is largely reflected in the statistical characteristics of the data as we shall see in Section 2.4.

Although the FX market consists of spot and longer term instruments, we concentrate here on the spot market[8] that operates mainly through electronic screens from financial news agencies like Reuter's, Knight Ridder or Telerate, where market makers enter quotes for their bid and ask prices. The actual deals are then made over the telephone. Transactions can also be made directly through automated dealing systems that offer the advantage of displaying actual transaction prices and volumes. Despite the growing importance of such markets[9], these transaction data became only very recently available to researchers in a quite limited amount[10]. As will be stated in Section (2.4.2), the properties of real transaction data do not differ from those of Reuter's FXFX data except for frequencies higher than 10 to 15 minutes. Therefore this survey concerns itself with tick-by-tick quoted prices from Reuter's FXFX page and equivalent service from Knight Ridder and Telerate[11]. To give an indication of the largest database of such quotes currently existing, Table 2.1 displays the number of quotes of the Olsen&Associates database on which some of the studies of this survey including the following chapters, were made. Table 2.1 also gives the average number of quotes available per FX rate. On the largest market, the USD/DEM, 4,500 quotes per day are available; that is, there is an average of 3 to 4 new quotes per minute, but this average can rise to 15-20 quotes per minute during the busiest periods.

An example of Reuter's FXFX page which displays constantly updated quotes from the banks that subscribe to its service is given in Table 2.2. A quoted price of 1.6290/00 for the USD-DEM rate expresses

Rate	Number of data	Businessday Frequency
USD_DEM	8,238,532	4,500
USD_JPY	4,230,041	2,300
GBP_USD	3,469,421	1,900
USD_CHF	3,452,559	1,900
USD_FRF	2,098,679	1,150
JPY_DEM	190,967	630
FRF_DEM	132,089	440
ITL_DEM	118,114	390
DEM_GBP	96,537	320
NLG_DEM	20,355	70

Table 2.1: Data Set

Number of data for the main FX rates against the USD (period 01.01.1987- 31.12.1993) and the DEM (period 01.10.1992-31.12.1993) using the filter for outliers of Dacorogna et al. (1994) .

the willingness of the market maker to buy USD at 1.6290 DEM, and sell USD at 1.6300 DEM. Actual trading prices and volumes are not known from this page. However reputation considerations prevent market makers from quoting prices at which they would actually not be willing to trade. Therefore real transaction prices will usually tend to be comprised within the quoted bid/ask spread (Petersen and Fialkowski, 1994).

In contrast to daily or weekly data, collecting these tick-by-tick quotes presents a number of practical problems such as transmission delays and breakdowns or aberrant quotes due to human and technical errors. Therefore, it is important to implement filters to eliminate outliers. The reader can find examples of such filters in Goodhart and Figliuoli (1991) and Dacorogna et al. (1993, 1994) . As noted in Dacorogna et al. (1994) , the percentage of quotes that are eliminated by

```
-----------------------------------------------------------------

0727 CCY PAGE NAME   * REUTER SPOT RATES * CCY    HI*EURO*LO FXFX
0727 DEM RABO RABOBANK UTR    1.6290/00  * DEM    1.6365    1.6270
0727 GBP MNBX MOSCOW   LDN    1.5237/42  * GBP    1.5245    1.5207
0727 CHF UBZA U B S    ZUR    1.3655/65  * CHF    1.3730    1.3630
0727 JPY IBJX I.B.J    LDN    102.78/83  * JPY    103.02    102.70
0727 FRF BUEX UE CIC   PAR    5.5620/30  * FRF    5.5835    5.5582
0726 NLG RABO RABOBANK UTR    1.8233/38  * NLG    1.8309    1.8220
0727 ITL BCIX B.C.I.   MIL 1592.00/3.00  * ITL    1596.00  1591.25
0727 ECU NWNT NATWEST  LDN    1.1807/12  * ECU    1.1820    1.1774

-----------------------------------------------------------------

XAU SBZG 387.10/387.60 * ED3  4.43/ 4.56 * FED    PREB * GOVA 30Y
XAG SBCM    5.52/ 5.53 * US30Y YTM  7.39 * 4.31- 4.31 * 86.14-15

-----------------------------------------------------------------
```

Table 2.2: Reuter's FXFX page screen

The first column gives the time (for example, for the first line, '07:27'), the second column gives the name of the currency ('DEM/USD'), the third column gives the name of the bank subsidiary which publishes the quote given as a mnemonic ('RABO' for the Rabobank), the fourth column gives the name of the bank ('Rabobank'), the fifth column gives the location of the bank as a mnemonic ('UTR' for Utrecht), the sixth and seventh column give the bid price with 5 digits ('1.6290') and the two last digits of the ask price ('00'), the last two columns give the highest ('1.6365') and the lowest ('1.6270') quoted prices of the day.

such filters is very low (less than 0.5%).

2.3 Definition of the Variables of Interest

Adequate analysis of such intradaily data relies on an explicit definition of the variables under study. Some of these definitions are *redefinitions* of variables in current everyday use, it must be stressed. These include the price, the change of price, the volatility and the spread. The remainder are newly developed variables, formulated to better capture the peculiarities of the intra-day market. These include the tick frequency, the

volatility ratio and the directional change frequency. An extensive notation is given along with the usual simplified notation to make all the
underlying parameters explicit. For each variable, we first give a formal
definition and then discuss its use.

2.3.1   Definition 1: the price

The *price* at time t, $x(\tau_j)$, is defined as

$$x(\tau_j) \quad \equiv \quad [\log p_{bid}(\tau_j) \; + \; \log p_{ask}(\tau_j)] \; / \; 2 \qquad\qquad (2.1)$$

where τ_j is the sequence of the tick recording times which is unequally
spaced. An alternative notation is

$$x(t_i) \quad \equiv \quad x(t_i, \Delta t) \quad \equiv \quad [\log p_{bid}(t_i) \; + \; \log p_{ask}(t_i)] \; / \; 2 \qquad (2.2)$$

where t_i is the sequence of the regular spaced in time data and Δt is the
time interval ($\Delta t = 1$ day, $\Delta t = 1$hour, ...).

Definition 1 takes the average of the bid and ask price rather than
either the bid or the ask series as a better approximation of the transaction price. Indeed as Fact 6 will point out, market makers frequently
skew the spread towards a more favourable price to offset their position.
In that context, the bid (or ask) price acts as a dummy value. Furthermore, in Definition 1, the average of the logarithms of the bid and
ask prices rather than the logarithm of the average is taken since the
former quantity has the advantage of behaving anti-symmetrically when
the price is inverted.

One important issue in the case of intradaily data is the use of the
right *time-scale*. Contrary to daily and weekly data, tick-by-tick data are
indeed irregularly spaced in time, τ_j. However, most statistical analyses
rely upon the use of data regularly spaced in time, t_i. For obtaining
price values at a time t_i within a data hole or in any interval between
ticks we use the linear interpolation between the previous price at τ_{j-1}
and next one at τ_j, with $\tau_{j-1} < t_i < \tau_j$. As advocated in Müller et
al. (1990), linear interpolation is the appropriate method for interpolat-
ing in a series with independent random increments for most types of

analyses. An alternative interpolation method might be to use the most recently published price as in Wasserfallen and Zimmermann (1985) although this introduces an inevitable bias in the data. However, as long as the data frequency is low enough, the results do not depend too much on the choice of either method. Although regularly time spaced data are used in most of the definitions below, irregularly time spaced data could alternatively be used by replacing t_i by τ_j. Finally, in addition to these two time-scales, other time-scales have been proposed to model characteristics of the intradaily FX market such as the seasonality (Dacorogna et al., 1993), the heteroskedasticity (Zhou, 1993) or both of them (Müller et al., 1993; Guillaume et al., 1996).

Another important issue is the definition of an *effective price*. Indeed, at frequencies higher than 10 minutes, the size of the spread is of the same order of magnitude as the size of the price changes. Moreover, the quoted spread does not exactly reflect the real spread, which is usually smaller as reported in Goodhart et al. (1994)[12]. Furthermore, because of transmission delays, it may be, for example, that market maker B enters a quote after market maker A, but that the quote of market maker B is the first to appear on the multi-contributor page of Reuters. Similarly, holes due to transmission breakdowns become more significant at such frequencies. Therefore, at frequencies higher than approximately 10 minutes, reliable analysis of prices can only be done on the basis of real transaction prices or with a thorough knowledge of the shortcomings of the database.

In the absence of such real transaction prices, we may define an effective price algorithm by looking at the properties of the prices and the market structure organisation. Assuming that quotes have a life-time of approximately 2 minutes during periods of average activity, one could take the best bid and ask quotes available in such a time window or the averages of the bids and of the asks. Another idea for such an algorithm would be to eliminate the negative first-order autocorrelation of the prices present at such frequencies (see Fact 5). An example of an algorithm for the computation of effective price is given in Bollerslev and Domowitz (1993) where the trade-matching algorithm designed for the interbank market by Reuters – Dealing 2000 system – is used. Interestingly, the prices generated by this algorithm exhibit a positive rather than negative first-order autocorrelation. In contrast, Goodhart et al. (1994) still obtain a negative first-order autocorrelation - although less pronounced - in their analysis of the Dealing 2000-2 system from Reuters.

2.3.2   Definition 2: the change of price

The *change of price* at time t_i, $r(t_i)$, is defined as

$$r(t_i) \quad \equiv \quad r(\Delta t; t_i) \quad \equiv \quad [x(t_i) \quad - \quad x(t_i - \Delta t)] \qquad (2.3)$$

where $x(t_i)$ is the sequence of equally spaced in time logarithmic price, and Δt is the fixed time-interval (10 minutes, 1 hour, 1 day, ...).

The change of the logarithmic price is often referred to as "return". It is usually preferred to the price itself as it is the variable of interest for traders maximising short term investment returns. Furthermore, its distribution is more symmetric than the distribution of the price. Finally, it is usually advocated that contrary to the price process which is clearly non-stationary, the process of the price changes should be stationary. Although unit root tests such as the Augmented Dickey Fuller test cannot reject the hypothesis of stationarity in the mean (Goodhart and Figliuoli, 1991), the autocorrelation of the volatility would probably cause the rejection of covariance stationarity by a test such as the one proposed in Loretan and Phillips (1994).

2.3.3   Definition 3: the volatility

The *volatility* at time t_i, $v(t_i)$, is defined as

$$v(t_i) \quad \equiv \quad v(\Delta t, S; t_i) \quad \equiv \quad \frac{1}{n} \sum_{k=1}^{n} |r(\Delta t; t_{i-k})| \qquad (2.4)$$

where S is the sample period on which the volatility is computed (for example 1 day or 1 year) and n is a positive integer with $S = n\Delta t$. A usual example is the computation of the daily volatility as the average daily volatility over one year ($S = 1$ year, $n = 250$ and $\Delta t = 1$ day). Note that in an autocorrelation study, for example, only 1 data point may be used ($S = \Delta t$) or n might be multiplied by a factor of 2 or 3 if overlapping data are taken as suggested in Müller (1993).

In Definition 3, the absolute value of the returns is preferred to the more usual squared value or more generally to any power ε ($\varepsilon \in R_o^+$) of $|r(\Delta t; t_i)|$. This is because the former quantity better captures the autocorrelation and the seasonality of the data (Taylor, 1988; Müller et al., 1990; Granger and Ding, 1993). This greater capacity to reflect the structure of the data can also be easily derived from the non-existence of a fourth moment in the distribution of the price changes (see Fact 4).

Although Definition 3 is the most appropriate for the assessment of risk or for forecasting, one might prefer other definitions of the volatility that give more weight to the tails of the distribution: for instance the cube root of the third moment for the evaluation of extreme downside risk in portfolio optimisation as in Roy (1952). One could also prefer the use of conditional volatility such as defined by the option model (Cox and Rubinstein, 1985) or the Generalised Autoregressive Conditional Heteroskedastic (GARCH) model (Bollerslev, 1986). However, although both approaches might appear appealing at the daily frequency, their use at the intradaily frequency presents important drawbacks: on the one side, the implicit volatility cannot be computed at very high frequency since options are not quoted at such frequencies; on the other side, as a consequence of the heterogeneity of the FX market, intradaily FX rates cannot be described by one homogeneous GARCH model (see Chapter 5).

2.3.4   Definition 4: the relative spread

The relative *spread* at time t_i, $s(t_i)$, is defined as

$$s(t_i) \equiv \log p_{ask}(t_i). - \log p_{bid}(t_i) \qquad (2.5)$$

Definition 4.1:

The *log spread* at time t_i, $\log s(t_i)$, is defined as

$$\log s(t_i) \equiv \log(\log p_{ask}(t_i) - \log p_{bid}(t_i)) \tag{2.6}$$

In the above definition, the relative spread $s(t_i)$ is preferred to the nominal spread $(p_{ask}(t_i) - p_{bid}(t_i))$ since it is dimensionless and can therefore be directly compared between different currencies. The spread of the inverse rate (e.g. JPY per USD instead of USD per JPY) is simply $-s(t_i)$, so that the variance of $s(t_i)$ is invariant under inversion of the rate.

It might however be sometimes preferable to study $\log s(t_i)$ instead of $s(t_i)$, because the former quantity has a more symmetric behaviour between low and high values. The relative spread is indeed a positive bounded quantity that has a skewed distribution function. It cannot be much lower than the typical value – that is, 10, 7, 5, or 15 basis points – but, on the positive side, it can exceed the typical value by a factor of 2 or more. Moreover, these high spreads which tend to numerically dominate a statistical analysis, usually occur in thin and unimportant markets, for example over the weekend or during the East Asian lunch break.

The spread is indicative of the transaction and inventory costs of the market maker who is under reputation consideration pressures. It is also affected by the degree of informational asymmetries and competitiveness. Thus, the spread depends both on the cost structure of the quoting bank and on the habits of the market. On the other side, it is the only source of cost for the traders since intradaily credit lines on the foreign exchange markets are free of interest[13].

2.3.5   Definition 5: the tick frequency

The *tick frequency* at time t_i, $f(t_i)$, is defined as

$$f(t_i) \equiv f(S; t_i) \equiv \frac{1}{S} N(\{x(\tau_j) \mid \tau_j \in (t_i - S, t_i]\}) \tag{2.7}$$

Definition 5.1:

The log *tick frequency* at time t_i, $\log f(t_i)$, is defined as

$$\log f(t_i) \equiv \log f(S; t_i) \tag{2.8}$$

where $N(\{x(t_j)\})$ is the counting function and S is the sample period on which the counting is computed. The alternative log form has been found to be more relevant in Demos and Goodhart (1992) .

The tick frequency is sometimes taken as a proxy for the transaction volume on the markets. As the name and location of the quoting banks are also given, the tick frequency is also sometimes disaggregated by bank. However, equating tick frequency to transaction volume or using it as a proxy for both volume and strength of bank presence suffers from the following problems: First, although it takes only a few seconds to enter a price quotation in the terminal, if two market makers happen to simultaneously enter quotes, only one quote will appear on the data collector's screen; Second, during periods of high activity, some operators may be too busy to enter the quote into the system; Third, a bank may use an automatic system to publish prices to advertise itself on the market. Conversely, well-established banks might not need to publish as many quotes on smaller markets; Fourth, the representation of the banks depends on the coverage of the market by data vendors such as Reuters or Knight Ridder. This coverage is changing and does not totally represent the whole market. For example, Asian market makers are not as well covered by Reuters as the Europeans. Asian market makers are instead more inclined to contribute to the more local financial news agencies such as Minex; Fifth, trading strategies of big banks are highly decentralised by subsidiary. Even between the back office and the trading room[14] or within the trading room itself, different traders may have completely different strategies.

2.3.6 Definition 6: the volatility ratio

The *volatility ratio* at time t_i, $Q(t_i)$, is defined as

$$Q(t_i) \equiv Q(\Delta t, n; t_i) \equiv \frac{|\sum_{k=1}^{n} r(t_{i+k})|}{\sum_{k=1}^{n} |r(t_{i+k})|} \tag{2.9}$$

The volatility ratio defined above is simply a generalisation of the variance ratio introduced in Lo and MacKinlay (1988) and Poterba and Summers (1988) where the absolute value of the price change instead of the variance is used as a measure of the volatility to take into account the statistical properties of the data (see Definition 3). The ratio can take values between "1" when the price changes follow a pure trend and "0" when they behave purely randomly.

The volatility ratio has been used in a variety of applications, including the effect of structural changes on prices, hypothesis testing in the empirical literature on the micro-structure of the markets and the identification of the nature of news. Here, however, we would like to stress the potential use of the volatility ratio as a general statistic to measure the trend-following behaviour of the price changes. This can be viewed as an alternative measure of the risk next to the volatility. Indeed, even though the two time series may have the same average volatility, the volatility ratio will be equal to "1" when the price changes follow a pure trend and to "0" when they behave randomly. Although the volatility ratio has many interesting features, we introduce a more precise statistic which seems to be more appealing to quantify the trend-following behaviour of the price changes.

2.3.7 Definition 7: the directional change frequency

The *directional change frequency* at time t_i, $d(t_i)$, is defined as

$$d(t_i) \equiv d(\Delta t, n, r_c; t_i) \equiv \frac{1}{n\Delta t} N(\{k | m_k \neq m_{k-1}, \ 1 < k \leq n\}) \quad (2.10)$$

where $N(\{k\})$ is the counting function, $n\Delta t$ the sampling period on which the counting is performed, m_k indicates the mode – upwards or downwards – of the current trend and r_c is a threshold value used to compute the change of mode. The directional change frequency, $d(t_i)$, is simply the frequency of significant mode (m_k) changes with respect to the latest extremum value (max_k or min_k) and a constant threshold value r_c^{15}.

In contrast with the definition of the volatility where the time interval is the arbitrarily set parameter and the amplitude of the change of price is the varying parameter, in the above formulation, the time is varying and the threshold is fixed. Thus, the definition also takes into account gradually occurring directional changes.

The directional change frequency is similar to the volatility ratio defined above in that they both measure the trend-following behaviour of the price changes and, as such, provide an alternative measure of the risk. However, unlike the volatility ratio, it is based on a threshold which is a measure of the risk quite natural to traders as put by one of them: "Although volatility can tell us the general environment of the market, we are actually more interested in the timing of our trades[16]. The knowledge of whether prices are likely to move more than a certain threshold allows us to decide when we need to close a position. The height of this threshold will vary according to our attitude towards risk." The use of thresholds and measures of trends is also very familiar to chartists (see, for example, the technique of Point and Figure Charts in Meyers (1989)).

2.4 Stylised facts

We can now consider a new set of stylised facts describing the characteristics of the FX market, and most importantly, how it functions. These facts have been grouped to show the distributional properties, the price formation process and the time series properties.

2.4.1 Distribution

The variety of opinions about the distributions of FX price changes and their generating process is wide. Some authors claim the distributions to be close to Paretian stable (McFarland et al., 1982), some to Student distributions (Boothe and Glassman, 1987), some reject any single distribution (Calderon-Rossel and Ben-Horim, 1982).

Instead of looking at the center of the distribution, an alternative way to characterise the distribution is to look at the tails. Most types of distributions can indeed be classified into 3 categories (de Haan, 1990) (de Haan, 1990): (i) Thin-tailed distributions for which all moments exist and whose cumulative distribution function declines exponentially in the tails; (ii) Fat-tailed distributions whose cumulative distribution function declines with a power in the tails; (iii) Bounded distributions which have no tails. A nice result is that these categories can be distinguished by the use of only one parameter, the tail index α with $\alpha = \infty$ for distributions of category (i), $\alpha > 0$ for category (ii) and $\alpha < 0$ for category (iii).

The empirical estimation of the tail index and the variance of this tail index crucially depends on the size of the sample. Indeed, for a given sample size, on the one hand, using too many observations introduces a bias in the tail index as some of the observations do not belong to the tail anymore but are from the center of the distribution; on the other hand, using too few observations introduces an inefficiency in the estimation of the variance of the tail index. Therefore, the very large sample size available with intradaily data ensures that enough tail observations are present in the sample.

An important result is that the tails of a fat-tailed distribution are invariant under addition although the distribution as a whole may vary according to temporal aggregation (Feller, 1971). That is, if weekly returns are Student-t identically and independently distributed, then monthly returns are not Student-t distributed[17]. Yet the tails of the monthly return distribution are like the tails of the weekly returns, with the same exponent α.

Another important result in the case of fat-tailed distributions concerns the existence of the moments of the distribution. Let X be the observed variable, c a scale variable and α the tail index. From

$$\mathrm{E}\,[\,X^k\,] \;=\; c\int_1^\infty x^{k-\alpha-1}dx \quad, \tag{2.11}$$

it is easily seen that only the first k-moments, $k < \alpha$, are bounded.

Finally, the tail index reflects the interaction of different agents on the markets. Indeed, the probability of extreme events depends on the

presence or absence of certain market participants such as medium-term
investors or pure speculators due to changing market conditions. The
mechanisms leading to these fat tails can be understood as follows:
whenever (relatively) long term traders become active following some
news or perturbation, shorter term traders become even more active
and tend to reinforce the longer term fluctuations, thereby creating fat
tails (see Fact 12). This is a kind of "cascade" effect where getting
over a particular threshold at one (long) time interval attracts exceed-
ings of thresholds at other time horizons. This cascade effect thus can
be explained by models of imperfect, though rational, information aggregation. In the absence of common information on the other traders'
preferences or beliefs on the impact of news, this will cause some learning
mechanism by the intra-day dealers before the prices fully incorporate
the new information. Here, we posit that the larger the tail index, the
less friction in the adjustment of prices to external shocks and the more
efficient the market will be. Indeed, since most fundamentals have thin
tails, a small tail index can only result from large fluctuations due to
the trading process.

Fact 1: Non stable, fat-tailed distribution

From Table 2.3, it appears that the main FX rates against the USD
have a tail index of ≈ 3.5, whereas the tail index for the EMS computed
rates against the DEM has a lower value of ≈ 2.7 and the tail index
for the DEM/JPY and GBP/DEM is even larger than for free-floating
rates against the USD. Quoted cross-rates in the EMS on the other hand
have an even smaller value, reflecting the upward bias of the results with
computed cross-rates at the 10 minutes interval due to the larger spread
(Dacorogna et al., 1994). This has the effect of gaussian noise. However,
the error bars of the tail index on quoted cross-rates are much larger
because of the small size of the sample for that exercise. The smaller tail
index for these rates thus indicates that the reduced variance induced by
the EMS set-up is at the cost of a larger probability of extreme events.

Table 2.3 indicates that FX rates belong to the class of fat-tailed

Rate	10m	30m	1h	6h
USD_DEM	3.11 ±0.33	3.35 ±0.29	3.50 ±0.57	4.48 ±1.64
USD_JPY	3.53 ±0.21	3.55 ±0.47	3.62 ±0.46	3.86 ±1.81
GBP_USD	3.44 ±0.22	3.52 ±0.46	4.01 ±1.09	6.93 ±10.79
USD_CHF	3.64 ±0.41	3.74 ±0.82	3.84 ±0.77	4.39 ±4.64
USD_FRF	3.34 ±0.22	3.29 ±0.47	3.40 ±0.69	4.61 ±1.21
FRF_DEM	3.11 ±0.41	2.55 ±0.23	2.43 ±0.23	3.54 ±1.42
DEM_NLG	3.05 ±0.27	2.44 ±0.08	2.19 ±0.12	3.37 ±1.43
DEM_ITL	3.31 ±0.51	2.93 ±1.17	2.54 ±0.49	2.86 ±0.98
GBP_DEM	3.68 ±0.35	3.63 ±0.42	4.18 ±1.17	3.22 ±0.79
DEM_JPY	3.96 ±0.41	4.18 ±0.90	4.13 ±1.05	4.71 ±1.61

Table 2.3: Estimated tail exponent

Estimated tail exponent α and its standard error for the main FX rates against the USD and some of the main (computed) cross-rates against the DEM. The results are taken from Dacorogna et al. (1994). The bias was estimated using a bootstrap method. In contrast to quoted cross-rates, computed cross-rates are obtained via the two bilateral rates against the USD. Their spread is thus approximately twice the normal spread.

non-stable distributions which have a finite tail index. Furthermore, estimations of the kurtosis of the FX rate returns for several time-intervals in Tables 2.4 and 2.5 in the appendix give additional evidence in favour of the non-stability of the FX rates distribution[18].

From Table 2.3, one can also verify the invariance of the tail index under aggregation, except for the longest intervals, mainly the 6 hour interval where the small number of data becomes a problem in getting significant estimates of α. The smaller number of data for large intervals forces the estimation algorithm to use a larger fraction of this data, closer to the center of the distribution. Thus the empirically measured tail properties become distorted by properties of the center of the distribution which, for $\alpha > 2$ and under aggregation, approaches the normal distribution (with $\alpha = \infty$) as a consequence of the central limit theorem.

Fact 2: Finite variance

Table 2.3 and Tables 2.4 and 2.5 in the appendix suggest that the variance exists for all currencies.

Fact 3: Symmetric distribution

It appears from Table 2.3 and Tables 2.4 and 2.5 in the appendix that the third moment exists and the distribution is symmetric for all FX rates but, possibly, the EMS cross-rates.

Fact 4: Decreasing leptokurticity

However, it appears from these tables that the fourth moment is not finite. Indeed, the larger the number of observations, the larger the kurtosis will be. At frequencies higher than 10 minutes, there seems to be some contradiction between the work of Goodhard and Figliuoli (1991) which claims that the leptokurticity starts to decrease at these frequencies, and the paper of Bollerslev and Domowitz (1993) which gives some evidence of a still increasing leptokurticity. One can show, however, that both results hold depending on whether one uses the linear interpolation method or the previous tick (see Definition 1 and below) to obtain price values at fixed time intervals at such frequencies. This is an example of the difficulty of making reliable analyses of quoted prices at frequencies higher than 10 minutes.

The absence of the fourth moment explains why the absolute value of the price changes has been found to be the best definition of the volatility, that is, the one which exhibits the strongest structure. Indeed, since the fourth moment of the distribution comes into the computation of the autocorrelation function of the variance, its structure will depend on the number of data points used.

2.4.2 Price formation process

The following three facts pertain to the short term (less than 10 minutes) behaviour of the foreign exchange intradaily price changes. It should be stressed that these facts characterise FXFX quotes as opposed to real transaction prices. They highlight the need for the definition of an effective price and the difficulties inherent to tick-by-tick analysis.

Fact 5: Negative first-order autocorrelation of the returns

Goodhart (1989) and Goodhart and Figliuoli (1991) first reported the existence of negative first-order autocorrelation of the price changes at the highest frequencies, which disappear once the price formation process is over. Goodhart (1989) also demonstrated that this negative auto-correlation is not affected by the presence (or absence) of major news announcements. Finally, Goodhart and Figliuoli (1992) showed that the resulting oscillations of the prices are not caused by bouncing prices between different geographical areas with different information sets. Note that this negative first-order auto-correlation of FXFX quotes is in constrast with the absence of such auto-correlation of real transaction prices, at least for the very small data sample studied in Goodhart et al. (1995).

A first explanation of this fact may be divergent opinions among traders. The conventional assumption that the FX market is composed of homogeneous traders who would share the same views about the effect of news, so that no correlation of the prices would be observed – or at most, a positive autocorrelation –. However, traders have diverging opinions about the impact of news on the direction of prices. A second – and complementary – explanation for this negative auto-correlation is the tendency of market makers to skew the spread in a particular direction when they have order imbalances (Bollerslev and Domowitz (1993) and Flood (1994)). A third explanation is that even without order imbalances or diverging opinions on the price, certain banks systematically publish higher bid/ask spreads than other. This could also cause the ask (bid) prices to bounce back and forth between banks (Bollerslev and Melvin, 1994).

Fact 6: Discreteness of spread

Quoted spreads are discretely distributed with the major peak being 10 basis points followed by the 5, 15 and 7 peaks. All together those peaks account for more than 97% of the distribution (Bollerslev and Melvin, 1994). These conventional spreads have also evolved over the years, depending on the markets, 10 rather than 20 basis points being the most quoted spread in recent years for example as the size of the price has become smaller (Müller and Sgier, 1992).

As explained in Definition 5 above, spreads mainly depend on the cost structure of the bank that is the market maker and on the habits of the market. As shown in Goodhart and Curcio (1991), individual banks usually quote two or three different spreads. When a market maker wants to push the price in a particular direction, he will tend to skew the spread in that direction but will use a spread of conventional size, generally 5 or 7; when he only wishes to trade or is uncertain about the direction the price should take, he will quote larger spreads with conventional values such as 10 or 15. Because different banks have different conventions, the distribution of spreads has 4 or 5 peaks instead of 2 or 3.

Note, once again, that the quoted spreads do not exactly reflect the transaction spread, which are usually smaller except for highly volatile periods (Goodhart et al., 1995a). Another difference is the continuous distribution (between 0 and 20 basis points) of transaction spreads.

Consistent with theory (Admati and Pfleiderer, 1988; Subrahmanyam, 1991) market makers will cover themselves by conventionally larger spreads in periods of higher risk such as the release of important news (Goodhart, 1989), the closing or opening of markets (Bollerslev and Domowitz, 1993) and lunch breaks (Müller et al., 1990). More generally, the amplitude of the spread is inversely related to expected market activity as measured by tick frequency or mean hourly volatility (Müller et al., 1990). The amplitude of the spread is directly related to the (instantaneous) volatility, which also measures the risk (Bollerslev and Domowitz, 1993).

Fact 7: Extremely short term triangular arbitrage

The building-up process of the prices in the very short run is also reflected in the significant predicting power of the USD/DEM relative to contrast to the other currencies (Goodhart and Figliuoli, 1991). A short delay is indeed needed before traders in smaller currencies adjust themselves to the patterns of the two leading currencies. Eben (1994) also finds evidence of triangular arbitrage opportunities at very high frequencies arising when very short-term trend reversals between two USD-rates are not yet reflected in the quoted cross-rates. Although the detection of triangular arbitrage opportunities is rather easy and quick with a unique unit of account or vehicle currency, it takes more time when the rates between two vehicles (USD and DEM) change (Suvanto, 1993). Finally, no study has yet showed whether such arbitrage opportunities are available with real transaction data.

2.4.3   Heterogeneous Structure

The following facts show that the diversity of the market participants described in the first part is reflected in geographically and institutionally differentiated behaviours and in the presence of agents acting within different time-horizons. They also illustrate the information flows between these different market components. Note that these facts pertain to FX rates at frequencies lower than 10 to 15 minutes. As such, they are thus independent of the indicative nature of FXFX quotes.

Fact 8: Seasonality

Although the FX market is virtually a global market, strong (deterministic) seasonal patterns corresponding to the hour of the day, the day of the week and the presence of the traders in the three major geographical trading zones can be observed. These seasonal patterns are found for all the five variables, the volatility (Bollerslev and Domowitz, 1993; Dacorogna et al., 1993), the relative spread (Müller and Sgier, 1992), the tick frequency (Goodhart and Demos, 1990; Müller et al., 1990),

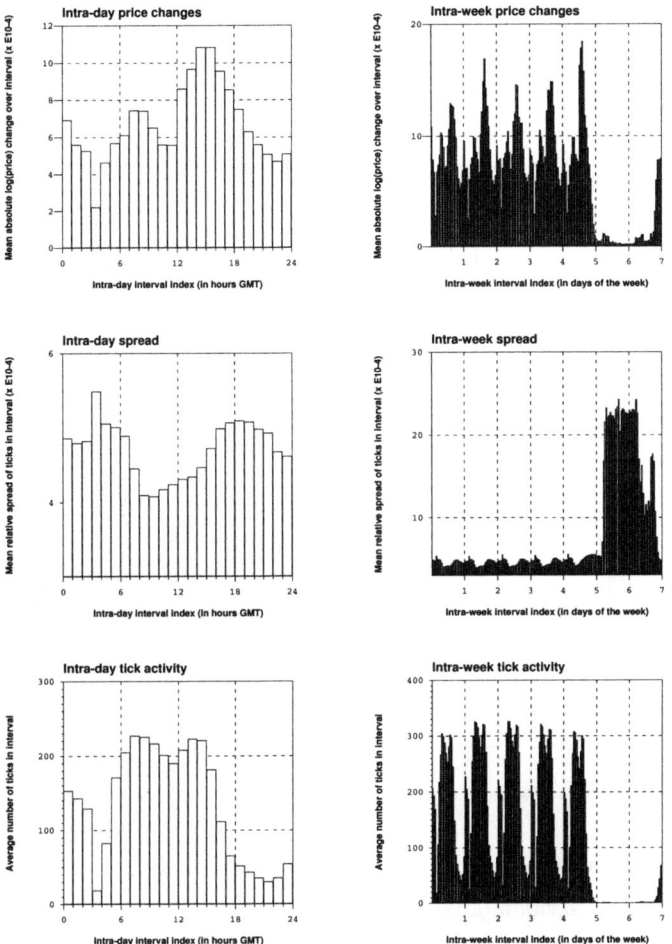

Figure 2.1: Hourly intra-day and intra-week distribution of the absolute price change, the spread and the tick frequency

A sampling interval of Δt = 1 hour is chosen. The day is subdivided into 24 hours from 0:00 - 1:00 to 23:00 - 24:00 (GMT) and the week is subdivided into 168 hours from Monday 0:00 - 1:00 to Sunday 23:00 - 24:00 (GMT) with index i. Each observation of the analysed variable is made in one of these hourly intervals and is assigned to the corresponding subsample with the correct index i. The sample pattern is independent of bank holidays and daylight saving time. The currency is the USD/DEM.

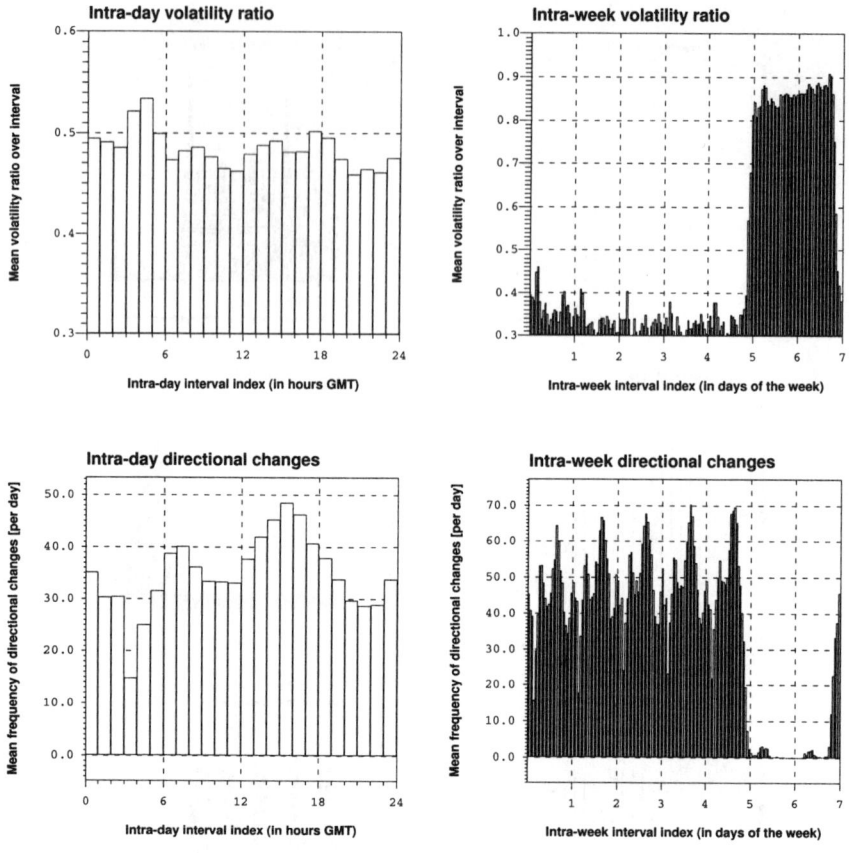

Figure 2.2: Hourly intra-day and intra-week distribution of the volatility ratio and the directional change frequency

The number of subintervals (per hour) is 10. The threshold value for the directional change frequency is 0.0003. A sampling interval of $\Delta t = 1$ hour is chosen. The day is subdivided into 24 hours from 0:00 - 1:00 to 23:00 - 24:00 (GMT) and the week is subdivided into 168 hours from Monday 0:00 - 1:00 to Sunday 23:00 - 24:00 (GMT) with index i. Each observation of the analyzed variable is made in one of these hourly intervals and is assigned to the corresponding subsample with the correct index i. The sample pattern is independent of bank holidays and daylight saving time. The currency is the USD/DEM.

the volatility ratio and the directional change frequency (see below, Figure 2.2).

As can be seen on Figures 2.1 and 2.2, trading activity picks up after midnight as the Tokyo and Sydney markets open with subsequent activity in Singapore and Hong Kong. The abrupt decline in arrivals at 4:00 GMT signals lunch-time in these markets. Market intensity remains strong in the afternoon Far Eastern trading session, and continues as Hong Kong and Singapore close and London and Frankfurt open. Some decline thereafter is observed until the opening in New York. Activity bounces back during the overlap of the New York and European markets, declining monotonically after New York closes and until the Far Eastern markets open again. Activity is regular over the five weekdays.

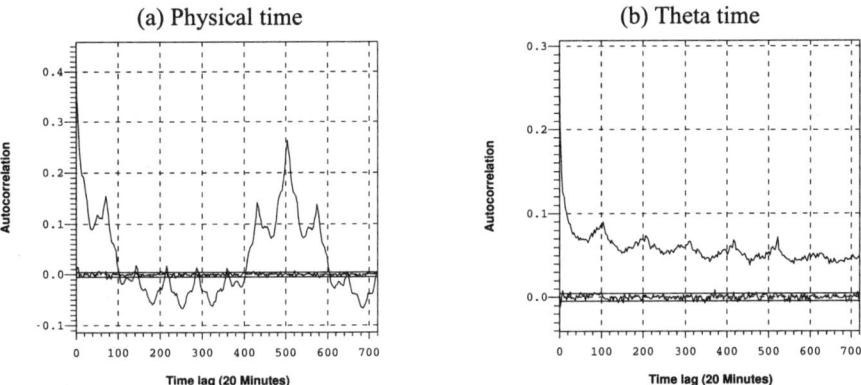

Figure 2.3: autocorrelation function for the absolute price changes

autocorrelation function for the absolute price changes in physical time with seasonal peaks (a) and in Theta-time (ϑ-time) with long memory effects (b) for the GBP/USD. The horizontal curve and the two horizontal lines around zero are, respectively, the autocorrelation function of the price changes and the 95% confidence interval. The ϑ-time scale basically expands periods of high activity and contracts periods of low volatility. The weekends and business holidays are thus virtually omitted by this ϑ-scale (Dacorogna et al., 1993).

With the exception of late Friday, which is already Saturday in the

Australian and Asian markets, there is no real discernable difference across the weekdays. The average activity is low on weekends, but higher on Sundays than on Saturdays. That may be due to the Middle Eastern markets, which can be open on Sundays and to early Monday morning activity in East Asia which coincides with Sunday nights. The seasonal patterns also appear in an autocorrelation study (see Figure 2.3(a)).

autocorrelation coefficients are indeed significantly higher for time lags that are integer multiples of the seasonal period than for other lags.

Although these seasonal patterns have similarities among all currencies, they can also be specific to a particular market. For CHF, for instance, there is a general spread increase with the high activity in America, while the average JPY spreads decrease at the same time. This indicates that American traders are less interested in CHF and more in JPY.

As shown in Chapter 5, the presence of these seasonal patterns introduces strong bias in the computation of simple statistics or the estimation of statistical processes with intradaily data. This can lead to spurious results when this seasonality is not taken care of, as is the case in many empirical studies on intradaily FX rates. There are however several ways to treat this seasonality. The first and most straightforward one is to introduce seasonal dummies as in Baillie and Bollerslev (1989). Another framework introduced in Andersen and Bollerslev (1996) is the use of a flexible Fourier framework to model the frequencies corresponding to the different seasonal peaks. A third possibility presented in Dacorogna et al. (1993) is the use of a different time scale, called Theta-time (ϑ-time). The ϑ-time scale expands daytimes having high mean volatilities and contracts daytimes having low volatilities and the weekends having very low volatilities. As can be seen from Figure 2.3(b), the deterministic seasonal patterns almost vanish with this new time scale.

Fact 9: Short and Long Term memory

The high short-term autocorrelation of the volatility and its clustering in periods of high volatility and low volatility are well-known since the work of Mandelbrot (1963). This motivated the introduction of the Autoregressive Conditional Heteroskedastic (ARCH) model by Engle (1982) and its generalised version (GARCH) by Bollerslev (1986), which have had much success (see Bollerslev et al. (1992)). More recently, it was found that the volatility also exhibits a very long-term memory characterised by an hyperbolic decline rather than the exponential decline of ARCH and GARCH processes. This lead to another generalisation of the GARCH model by Baillie et al. (1993), namely the Fractionally Integrated GARCH (FIGARCH).

Intradaily studies not only confirm the presence of these short- and long-term memories for the volatility (Dacorogna et al., 1993) (see Figure 2.3(b)) but also for other variables such as the spread (Müller and Sgier, 1992), the volatility ratio and the directional change frequency.

Furthermore, the analysis of intradaily data gives some insights on the origin of these clusters. One possibility is indeed the clustering of the arrival of news with the markets adjusting perfectly and instantaneously to the news. This is, however, not the reality as will be pointed out in Fact 14. Another possibility lies in the learning process of traders with different priors who may take some hours of trading to resolve their expectational differences after the arrival of important news. This would result in volatility spillovers that could either extend to other geographical trading areas or be restricted to their own market. Taking analogies from meteorology, Engle et al. (1990, 1992) called country-specific shocks a "heat wave" and the transmission of news across markets a "meteor shower". Due to their limited (daily) data set, Engle et al. (1990,1992) only found evidence of meteor showers. However, using hourly data, Baillie and Bollerslev (1989) conclude to the presence of both the heat wave and the meteor shower phenomena. Further evidence is also given in Figure 2.3(b): on the one side, the continuously high short-term autocorrelation is responsible for the meteor shower;

on the other side, the peaks at time lags corresponding to 1, 2 and 3 business days are evidence of the heat wave phenomenon. In addition to the presence of country-specific news, this heat wave could also be explained by the learning process of traders within a market. As one trader in the European market puts it, "when we arrive in the morning, we first take the temperature of the markets by reading the news, analysing the price levels and inquiring about the mood of other traders. To complete a strategy for the day, we integrate customer orders and technical resistance and support levels. Only then we start with trading and may close positions before lunch-time or before the announcement of important news." The response of traders to several different autocorrelated news arrival processes corresponding to different time-horizons is also a potential explanation for the long-term memory of the markets (Haubrich and Lo, 1992).

Fact 10: Fractal Structure

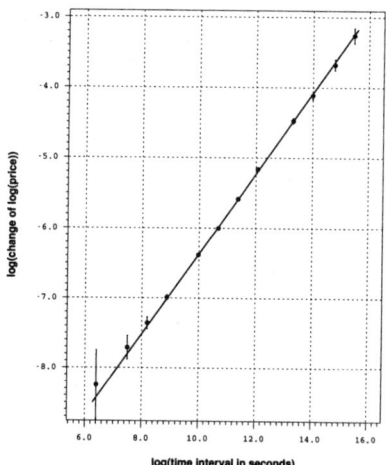

Figure 2.4: Scaling Law for the volatility

This figure gives the scaling law for the volatility for intervals extending from 10 minutes to two months. The currency is the USD/JPY.

Another very striking fact is the regular fractal structure of the FX rates in the sense of Mandelbrot (1983)[19]. This is illustrated by the scaling laws reported for the volatility and the directional change frequency.

The scaling law for the volatility (Müller et al., 1990) relates the volatility over a time interval Δt (see Definition 3) to the size of this interval :

$$v(\Delta t, S; t_i) = \left(\frac{\Delta t}{\Delta T} \right)^{\frac{1}{E}} \tag{2.12}$$

where S is the sampling period and ΔT is a constant depending on the FX rate. If Δt is expressed in days, ΔT is in the order of magnitude of 10^4 for the main FX rates against the USD. The drift exponent $1/E$ is about 0.58 for the major FX rates, compared to the $1/E = 0.5$ implying a pure gaussian random walk model.

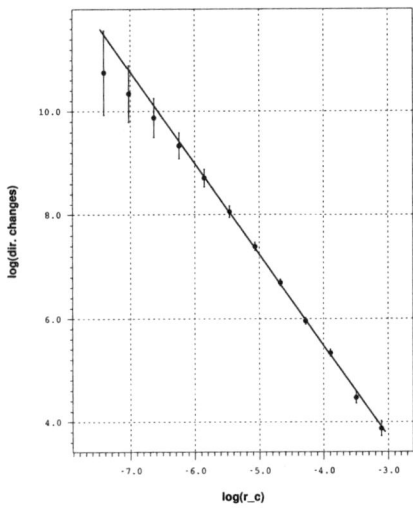

Figure 2.5: Scaling Law for the directional change

This figure gives the scaling law for the number of directional changes (see Definition 7) starting from threshold values of the size of the spread to the higher threshold values taken in a geometric progression. The currency is the USD/JPY.

A similar law relates the number of directional changes to the size of the threshold r_c :

$$S.d(S, r_c; t_i) \; = \; \left(\frac{r_c}{R}\right)^{\frac{1}{D}} \tag{2.13}$$

where S is the sampling period and R is a constant depending on the FX rate. The drift exponent $1/D$ is about -1.75 for the major FX rates, whereas a pure gaussian random walk model would imply $1/D = -2.0$. Both scaling laws were estimated by least squares.

The scaling laws expressed in equations 2.12 and 2.13 hold for all time series studied and for a wide variety of time intervals – from 10 minutes to 2 months – or threshold values as shown in Figures 2.4 and 2.5. Even more interestingly, recall that the definition of the directional change frequency is symmetric to the definition of the volatility: the volatility measures the variability of the price changes as a function of a fixed time interval whereas the directional change frequency measures the variability of the price changes as a function of fixed amplitude or threshold. Then, taking the inverse of the drift exponent in the scaling law for the directional change frequency, we should get a value similar to the value of the drift exponent in the scaling law for the volatility; this is indeed approximately the case after taking care of the negative slope.

Although no theoretical models yet provide an explanation, a highly tentative economic interpretation of this scaling law is that it represents a mix of risk profiles of agents trading at different time horizons. The average volatility on one horizon is indeed the maximum return a trader can expect to make on average at that horizon. Alternatively, the average number of directional changes for a particular threshold or return is the maximum number of profitable trades a trader can expect to make on average. As shown in Figure 2.6(a), this relationship between traders with different risk or time-horizon profiles is quite stable over the years, notwithstanding the tripling of the volume on the FX markets.

Fact 11: Institutional Framework

Intradaily analysis of FX rates within the European Monetary System (EMS) gives some insights on the distinct characteristics of the EMS system when the bands were still quite narrow. As illustrated in Figure 2.4.3, it achieved a smaller average volatility, represented by a value of the drift exponent of the scaling law much smaller than the average for free-floating currencies. Though, the value of its drift exponent went up to the average value for free floating currencies when the ITL left the EMS in 1992 and when the bands were broadened in 1993 in the case of the FRF.

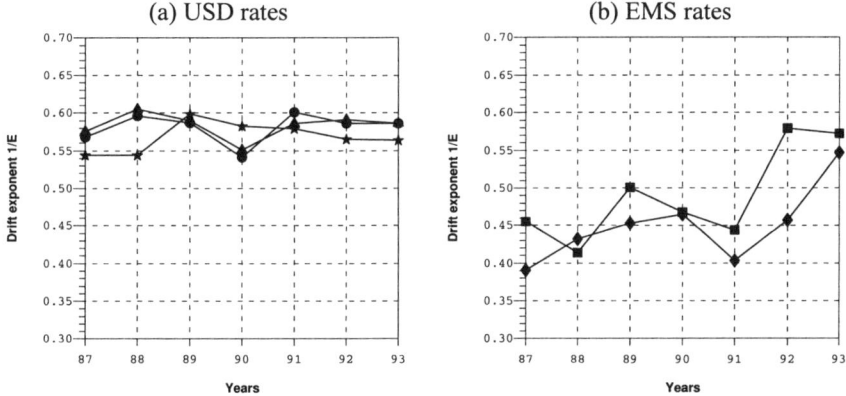

Figure 2.6: Drift exponent as a function of time

Yearly estimation of the drift exponent of the scaling law (see Fact 10) is given for USD rates on the left (DEM (circle), FRF (triangle), JPY (star)) (Figure (a)) and EMS rates against the DEM on the right (ITL (box) and FRF (diamond)) (Figure (b)).

The earlier volatility was achieved however at the cost of a much larger probability of extreme events as indicated by the smaller value of the tail index of EMS currencies in comparison with free-floating currencies (see Table 2.3 in Fact 1). This statistical characteristic demonstrates the low credibility of the former EMS' bands during our sample period (01.10.1992-31.12.1993) and shows that different institutional setups like the EMS can be distinguished by distinct and robust, model or process-independent, features[20].

Fact 12: Conditional predictability

The co-existence of different types of traders might be why conditional forecasts are possible although the price changes are globally unpredictable (see Fact 15). Based on earlier work by LeBaron (1992), Müller et al. (1994) show that tomorrow's volatility on a very short time horizon (for example 1 hour) can be systematically predicted by the volatility on a longer time-horizon (for example 1 day). This fact seems to indicate that the impact of important news first affects middle-term traders (over 1 day) and then propagate itself to short-term (intra-day) traders, who have to absorb the shock by a more intense activity. On the other hand, a more intense activity between intradaily dealers will not cause trend in the relatively longer run to appear. This is in line with the fact that most of the intradaily volume is made on the basis of "hot potato's" exchanged between different intradaily dealers (Lyons, 1997). These findings illustrate once again the change of dynamics for different types of volatility and the importance of information flows between clearly distinct types of traders.

Fact 13: Positive impact of official interventions

One type of trader that is of special interest is the central banks as the time and the size of their interventions can be measured on an intradaily basis. Central banks may operate either directly through officially announced interventions, indirectly through unannounced interventions or through big banks which represent a larger share of the market. Official interventions operate essentially as signals given to the markets and are therefore difficult to measure (see Edison (1993) for a review of the literature on central bank interventions).

Some evidence is given in Goodhart and Hesse (1993) that in the long run, official interventions would affect FX rates in the desired direction although they may result in short term losses for the central bankers.

One could, however, easily extend the analysis to any other long-term trader - that is, a trader who can afford a large open position - provided he has some impact on the market through his reputation even if he does not have a large share of the market. For example, this may be the case of some hedge funds. Peiers (1997) shows the positive impact of indirect interventions of the Bundesbank through the biggest player on the DEM/USD market, namely the Deutsche Bank.

Fact 14: Mixed effect of news

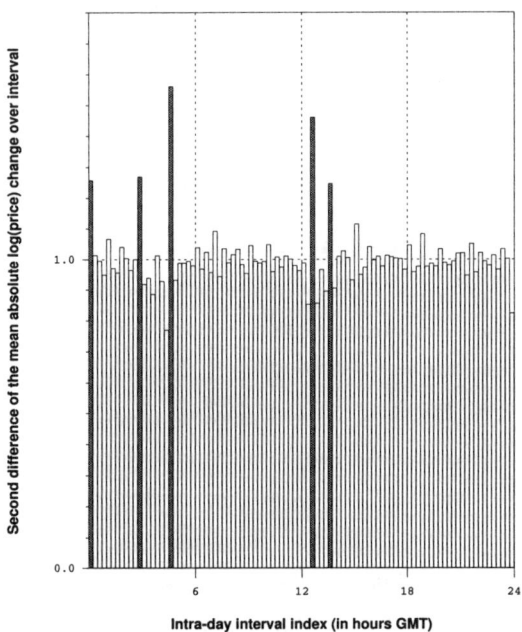

Figure 2.7: Intraday distribution per 15 minutes interval

Intraday distribution per 15 minutes interval of the second difference of the mean absolute price changes for the USD/DEM ($h_i = \exp[\ln |r_i| - \frac{1}{2} \ln |r_{i-1} r_{i+1}|]$). Sudden peaks are in darkened.

News is a very broad concept covering a phone call of a customer who wants to make a very large FX transaction (due to, say, inventory imbalances), a conversation with a colleague, price forecasts and histories when used in technical analysis programs or the economic forecasts of the research department of a bank, general economic and political news and major economic news announcements. news is therefore very difficult to quantify.

A first attempt to quantify news taken in Goodhart (1989) was to look at the 'news' pages of Reuters. General economic and political news are displayed on the AAMM page. Goodhart (1989) found out that unimportant news does not have a significant effect on the behaviour of the foreign exchange rates. Distinct and relatively large price movements unrelated to any news are indeed apparent. The price formation process seems to be independent of the presence or absence of news.

In contrast, major economic news announcements such as trade, unemployment, budget deficit or gross domestic product growth have significant impacts (Goodhart, 1989). Economic news announcements along with the market expectations and the effect of the previous announcement are displayed in Reuters' FXNB page. Effective news – that is, the difference between the markets expectation and the actual figure that is released – increase the volatility as the dispersion of traders' views on the impact of the effective news widens. The three right peaks in Figure 2.7 show the clearcut effect of this news release in New York and Japan. The two peaks for the US reflect the change of time with the Daylight Saving Time, which does not exist in Japan. The first two peaks on the left correspond to the beginning of the Japanese trading session and of the Japanese lunch respectively. Goodhart et al. (1993) further shows that major economic news announcement such as release of US trade figures or changes in the UK base interest rate have a significant impact on the price changes process. This effect is, however, temporary (3 to 4 days) as markets eventually incorporate the effects of the news. Moreover the direction of the effect on the level of the price is difficult to predict. This can be explained by the highly nonlinear dynamics of the FX rates (see Chapter 4)

An alternative way to quantify the impact of news derives from the mixture of distribution hypothesis (see Clark (1973), Tauchen and Pitts (1983) and Andersen (1992)) . In this framework, the clustering of the volatility results from the clustering of the news arrival process. Since the news arrival process is an unobserved variable, proxies for the market activity such as the volume of trade are used. Volume as such is however not available in the FX markets (see Section 5.2). Moreover, as shown in Jones et al. (1991), volume can be rather noisy. Therefore, empirical studies in the FX intradaily markets use the tick frequency and/or the spread as proxies for the level of activity. Although a certain correlation between these variables and the volatility is obvious from the simple inspection of Figure 2.1 in Fact 5 above, severe limitations harm the use of these variable as noted in Section 5.2. Moreover Davé (1993) shows that tick frequency can only be a good approximation of the volume when markets are analyzed as separate geographical entities - thus, when there is no overlap between markets and the data are not disaggregated by individual bank subsidiary. Goodhart (1989) also shows that tick frequency does not specifically rise when news are released. Anyhow, empirical evidence in favor of this mixture of distribution hypothesis is only partial (Bollerslev and Domowitz, 1993; Demos and Goodhart, 1992).

Fact 15: Highly complex system

As implied by the presence of a unit root (Goodhart and Figliuoli, 1992), FX price changes appear to be highly unpredictable. Though, at the same time, their dynamics is highly nonlinear (see Chapter 4) and, at least partly, endogenous as highlighted by Fact 14. This endogeneity of the price movements results from the information flow between agents trading within different geographical markets and time-horizons.

Since this endogeneity, together with the nonlinearity and the unpredictability, is the characteristic of a chaotic system, an interesting property to investigate is the degree of complexity of this chaotic system. A low-degree of complexity would indicate that the FX rates dynamics can mainly be described by an endogenous system with some small stochastic perturbations. Rather than the news itself, it is the complex nonlinear interaction and learning process of traders that would be responsible for the large and unpredictable movements of FX rates (DeGrauwe and Dewachter, 1993). Using a very large number of intradaily data over a sufficiently long period, we show in Chapter 3 that FX rates are a highly complex system.

Together with Fact 14, this fact implies that the dynamics of the FX markets cannot be simply explained by either the impact of one news process or the endogenous learning process of traders. More systematic relationships between the FX rates and the fundamentals or the news can probably only be detected by first trying to isolate the different components of the markets corresponding to different types of traders.

2.5 Conclusion

Looking through the microscope at the intradaily FX market, we have access to much more information than at lower frequencies such as daily or weekly. Not only is the number of data points 100 to 1000 times larger, other types of information such as news screens or new quantities are now available. This information set is highly interesting as it is the one used by intradaily traders who make up by far the largest share of the market (Bank of International Settlement, 1993). Its analysis also offers answers to several old debates and poses new challenges.

A first issue is the definition of an effective price at the extremely high frequency to replace transaction prices. Indeed, in the absence of widely available transaction prices, an effective price algorithm could be devised on the basis of the characteristics of the price formation process and the market structure organisation.

A second and somewhat related issue is the definition of the relevant time-scale. Contrary to traditionally available data, ticks are irregular spaced in physical time. Moreover, the heterogeneity of the markets causes inconsistencies in the estimation of models in physical time. Therefore, several alternative time-scales were suggested.

A third issue is the definition of the concept of risk. risk is traditionally defined by the volatility as measured by the variance and the co-variance. However, the absolute value of the returns is a more accurate definition of the volatility due to the non-existence of the fourth moment of the distribution. The tail index is another measure of risk which can be more accurate than the variance and co-variance. The analysis of EMS FX rates indeed showed that a reduced volatility does not necessarily imply a lower risk as measured by the tail index.

A fourth challenge is the definition of market efficiency and the related issue of the learning process of traders. The need for a dynamic definition of the concept of market efficiency is stressed by the mixed impact of news on the price changes on the one hand, and the spillover effects both across markets and across time-horizons on the other hand. This dynamic view of market efficiency does not preclude the possibility of conditional forecasting of the price changes as it explicitly takes into account the heterogeneity of the markets. Rather than the instantaneous adjustment of the price to news, market efficiency can now be defined as the smoothness of this adjustment process. In this perspective, appropriate measures of market efficiency could be the size of the spread or the tail index.

With respect to the heterogeneous behaviour of the traders, a fifth challenge is the definition of the right modelling approach to the markets. The short-comings of both the macro-economic and the time-series methodologies adopted so far have been highlighted. A first alternative may reside in the analysis of the sub-components of the markets rather than the market as a whole by using, for example, other time-scales corresponding to the time-horizon of a specific category of traders. A second alternative is the analysis of a particular category of traders whose specific time-horizon and objective function can be identified, like individual traders who would communicate the record of their trading. A third alternative would be to broaden the conceptual framework of the theoretical literature on the micro-structure of the markets to include traders with different time-horizons or geographical locations for example. Without taking this heterogeneity of the markets into account, it may prove extremely difficult if not impossible to find relationships between the price changes and the fundamentals or more generally the news arrival processes. For example, even the simple geographical dispersion of the different markets proves to be of prime importance for the consistent estimation of simple statistics or statistical models.

Finally, some light was shed on the old debate on the distribution of FX returns which was shown to belong to the class of fat-tailed non-stable distributions. Furthermore, the existence of the three first moments of the distribution for free-floating currencies was confirmed.

Footnotes

(1) For surveys on the FX market at the daily or weekly frequencies, see, for example, the surveys of Mussa (1979), Hsieh (1988), Baillie and McMahon (1989), de Vries (1994) .

(2) Holidays and business hours for the different markets can be found in Morgan (1994) .

(3) East Asia comprises Australia, Hong Kong, India, Indonesia, Japan, South Korea, Malaysia, New Zealand, Singapore. Europe comprises Austria, Bahrain, Belgium, Germany, Denmark, Finland, France, Great Britain, Greece, Ireland, Italy, Israel, Jordan, Kuwait, Luxembourg, Netherlands, Norway, Saudi Arabia, South Africa, Spain, Sweden, Switzerland, Turkey, United Arab Emirates. America comprises Argentina, Canada, Mexico, USA.

(4) Standard abbreviations of the International Organization for Standardization (ISO, code 4217).

(5) Net-net turnover; that is, adjusted for both local and cross-border double-counting.

(6) The high leverage and unregulated aspects of hedging funds distinguish their investors from other institutional investors.

(7) For example, Bank Negara of Malaysia was one of the most aggressive (short-term) speculators in the FX market for several years.

(8) The spot market accounted for 47% of the FX market in 1992 (Bank for International Settlements, 1993).

(9) In the United States and the United Kingdom, the share of deals going through such systems in April 1992 was 32 and 28% respectively (Bank for International Settlements, 1993).

(10) (Lyons, 1996b; Lyons, 1995; Lyons, 1996a; Lyons, 1997) and Goodhart et al. (1994) could exceptionally get respectively one week and one day of such data.

(11) See Danielsson and Payne (1999) for a comparison between Reuters' FXFX system and Reuters D-2002 electronic system.

(12) In their one day study of real transaction prices, Goodhart et al. (1994) found that although the actual spread is usually within the quoted spread, it could be larger in highly volatile periods.

(13) A trader taking a forward position overnight will of course have to pay the interest on his position between the trade and the settlement as well as the spread on the interest rate.

(14) The back office usually takes longer term positions than traders in the trading room who might not be allowed to take positions overnight.

(15) Appendix 2 gives a more detailed definition of the directional change frequency and a schematic example of its implementation.

(16) By trade, we mean entering *and* closing a position.

(17) This is an implication of the central limit law.

(18) Simulations in McCulloch (1994) and Gielens et al. (1995) show that one cannot univoquely distinguish between a fat-tailed non-stable and a thin-tailed distribution only on the basis of low estimated values of the tail index. However, the estimations of the kurtosis point in favour of the non-stability of the FX rates distribution.

(19) The fractal structure of the FX rates does not correspond to a

fractional brownian motion since the distribution is non stable. It is also more complex than the structure of a low-dimensional fractal attractor as illustrated by Fact 15.

(20) See Svensson (1992) for a review of the literature on the modeling of Target Zones, and in particular, of the EMS.

2.6 Appendix

2.6.1 Appendix 1

rate	time interval	mean	variance	skewness	kurtosis
USD/DEM	10 minutes	$-2.73 \cdot 10^{-7}$	$2.62 \cdot 10^{-7}$	0.17	35.10
	1 hour	$-1.63 \cdot 10^{-6}$	$1.45 \cdot 10^{-6}$	0.26	23.55
	6 hours	$-9.84 \cdot 10^{-6}$	$9.20 \cdot 10^{-6}$	0.24	9.44
	24 hours	$-4.00 \cdot 10^{-5}$	$3.81 \cdot 10^{-5}$	0.08	3.33
	1 week	$-2.97 \cdot 10^{-4}$	$2.64 \cdot 10^{-4}$	0.18	0.71
USD/JPY	10 minutes	$-9.42 \cdot 10^{-7}$	$2.27 \cdot 10^{-7}$	-0.18	26.40
	1 hour	$-5.67 \cdot 10^{-6}$	$1.27 \cdot 10^{-6}$	-0.09	25.16
	6 hours	$-3.40 \cdot 10^{-5}$	$7.63 \cdot 10^{-6}$	-0.05	11.65
	24 hours	$-1.37 \cdot 10^{-4}$	$3.07 \cdot 10^{-5}$	-0.15	4.81
	1 week	$-9.61 \cdot 10^{-4}$	$2.27 \cdot 10^{-4}$	-0.27	1.30
GBP/USD	10 minutes	$-6.91 \cdot 10^{-9}$	$2.38 \cdot 10^{-7}$	0.02	27.46
	1 hour	$7.61 \cdot 10^{-7}$	$1.40 \cdot 10^{-6}$	-0.23	21.53
	6 hours	$4.63 \cdot 10^{-6}$	$8.85 \cdot 10^{-6}$	-0.34	10.09
	24 hours	$1.72 \cdot 10^{-5}$	$3.60 \cdot 10^{-5}$	-0.26	4.41
	1 week	$6.99 \cdot 10^{-5}$	$2.72 \cdot 10^{-4}$	-0.66	2.77
USD/CHF	10 minutes	$-2.28 \cdot 10^{-7}$	$3.07 \cdot 10^{-7}$	-0.04	23.85
	1 hour	$-1.37 \cdot 10^{-6}$	$1.75 \cdot 10^{-6}$	0.05	18.28
	6 hours	$-8.23 \cdot 10^{-6}$	$1.11 \cdot 10^{-5}$	0.05	7.73
	24 hours	$-3.38 \cdot 10^{-5}$	$4.51 \cdot 10^{-5}$	-0.04	2.81
	1 week	$-2.58 \cdot 10^{-4}$	$3.16 \cdot 10^{-4}$	0.09	0.34
USD/FRF	10 minutes	$-1.98 \cdot 10^{-7}$	$2.08 \cdot 10^{-7}$	0.35	43.31
	1 hour	$-1.18 \cdot 10^{-6}$	$1.28 \cdot 10^{-6}$	0.47	28.35
	6 hours	$-7.13 \cdot 10^{-6}$	$8.29 \cdot 10^{-6}$	0.23	9.69
	24 hours	$-2.91 \cdot 10^{-5}$	$3.40 \cdot 10^{-5}$	0.06	3.22
	1 week	$-2.32 \cdot 10^{-4}$	$2.44 \cdot 10^{-4}$	0.16	0.88

Table 2.4: Price change distribution for main currencies against the USD

This table gives four first moments of the price change distribution at different time intervals for the major currencies against the USD.

rate	time interval	mean	variance	skewness	kurtosis
DEM/FRF	10 minutes	$9.84 \cdot 10^{-8}$	$1.91 \cdot 10^{-8}$	0.54	86.29
	1 hour	$5.89 \cdot 10^{-7}$	$1.14 \cdot 10^{-7}$	0.79	69.70
	6 hours	$3.53 \cdot 10^{-6}$	$6.53 \cdot 10^{-7}$	1.41	36.87
	24 hours	$1.07 \cdot 10^{-5}$	$2.84 \cdot 10^{-6}$	1.15	24.26
	1 week	$8.94 \cdot 10^{-5}$	$1.93 \cdot 10^{-6}$	1.92	3.95
DEM/NLG	10 minutes	$-5.19 \cdot 10^{-8}$	$1.42 \cdot 10^{-9}$	-5.68	9640.85
	1 hour	$-3.11 \cdot 10^{-7}$	$7.54 \cdot 10^{-9}$	2.76	4248.12
	6 hours	$-1.86 \cdot 10^{-6}$	$2.48 \cdot 10^{-8}$	0.74	124.35
	24 hours	$-7.80 \cdot 10^{-6}$	$9.66 \cdot 10^{-8}$	-0.30	30.02
	1 week	$-4.57 \cdot 10^{-5}$	$6.63 \cdot 10^{-7}$	0.03	0.06
DEM/ITL	10 minutes	$1.07 \cdot 10^{-6}$	$1.75 \cdot 10^{-7}$	0.86	64.03
	1 hour	$6.46 \cdot 10^{-6}$	$1.24 \cdot 10^{-6}$	1.83	89.92
	6 hours	$3.88 \cdot 10^{-5}$	$7.16 \cdot 10^{-6}$	1.03	37.26
	24 hours	$1.18 \cdot 10^{-4}$	$2.53 \cdot 10^{-5}$	-0.51	13.08
	1 week	$9.42 \cdot 10^{-4}$	$1.37 \cdot 10^{-4}$	-0.25	0.17
GBP/DEM	10 minutes	$4.53 \cdot 10^{-7}$	$9.86 \cdot 10^{-8}$	-0.32	25.97
	1 hour	$2.69 \cdot 10^{-6}$	$7.12 \cdot 10^{-7}$	-0.34	16.90
	6 hours	$1.56 \cdot 10^{-5}$	$4.62 \cdot 10^{-6}$	-0.02	7.48
	24 hours	$7.04 \cdot 10^{-5}$	$1.79 \cdot 10^{-5}$	0.27	3.15
	1 week	$1.17 \cdot 10^{-4}$	$1.29 \cdot 10^{-4}$	0.07	0.59
DEM/JPY	10 minutes	$-3.39 \cdot 10^{-6}$	$2.21 \cdot 10^{-7}$	-0.09	12.35
	1 hour	$-2.03 \cdot 10^{-5}$	$1.46 \cdot 10^{-6}$	-0.03	88.58
	6 hours	$-1.21 \cdot 10^{-4}$	$9.12 \cdot 10^{-6}$	-0.04	6.57
	24 hours	$-4.85 \cdot 10^{-4}$	$3.56 \cdot 10^{-5}$	0.12	2.52
	1 week	$-3.15 \cdot 10^{-3}$	$2.67 \cdot 10^{-4}$	-0.07	0.03

Table 2.5: Price change distribution for the main currencies against the DEM

This table gives four first moments of the price change distribution at different time intervals for the major currencies against the DEM.

2.6.2 Appendix 2

A more detailed definition of the *directional change frequency* at time t_i, $d(t_i)$, is as

$$d(t_i) \equiv d(\Delta t, n, r_c; t_i) \equiv \frac{1}{n\Delta t} \, N(\{k \mid m_k \neq m_{k-1}, 1 < k \leq n\}) \quad (2.14)$$

with the recursive variables m_k, which indicate the mode – upwards or downwards – of the current trend, and min_k (max_k), which indicate the minimum (maximum) value used as a reference to compute potential changes of mode. Formally, we have:

$$m_k = \begin{cases} 0, & k = 0 \\ \left. \begin{cases} +1 & \text{if } ((m_{k-1} \neq +1) \wedge (x(t_{i-n+k}) - min_{k-1} > r_c)) \\ -1 & \text{if } ((m_{k-1} \neq -1) \wedge (max_{k-1} - x(t_{i-n+k}) > r_c)) \\ m_{k-1} & \text{otherwise} \end{cases} \right\}, & k = 1, ..., n \end{cases}$$

$$max_k = \begin{cases} x(t_{i-n+k}) & \text{if } (k = 0) \vee [(m_k = 1) \wedge (m_{k-1} \neq 1)] \\ \max(max_{k-1}, x(t_{i-n+k})) & \text{otherwise} \end{cases}$$

$$min_k = \begin{cases} x(t_{i-n+k}) & \text{if } (k = 0) \vee [(m_k = -1) \wedge (m_{k-1} \neq -1)] \\ \min(min_{k-1}, x(t_{i-n+k})) & \text{otherwise} \end{cases}$$

where the computation sequence is $m_0, max_0, min_0, m_1, max_1, min_1, ...$ and where $N(\{k\})$ is the counting function, $n\Delta t$ the sampling period on which the counting is performed and r_c is a threshold value. The directional change frequency, $d(t_i)$, is simply the frequency of significant mode (m_k) changes with respect to the latest extremum value (max_k or min_k) and a constant threshold value r_c.

The threshold, r_c, should be related to the time frequency ($1/\Delta t$) at which the price change is taken and to the mean absolute value of the price change for this time interval Δt. On the one hand, the value of r_c should be large enough not to measure "noise" and, on the other hand, r_c should also reflect the typical sensitivity level of a trader operating at the corresponding time-horizon Δt. The scaling law described in Fact 7 may represent a possibility of linking r_c to Δt.

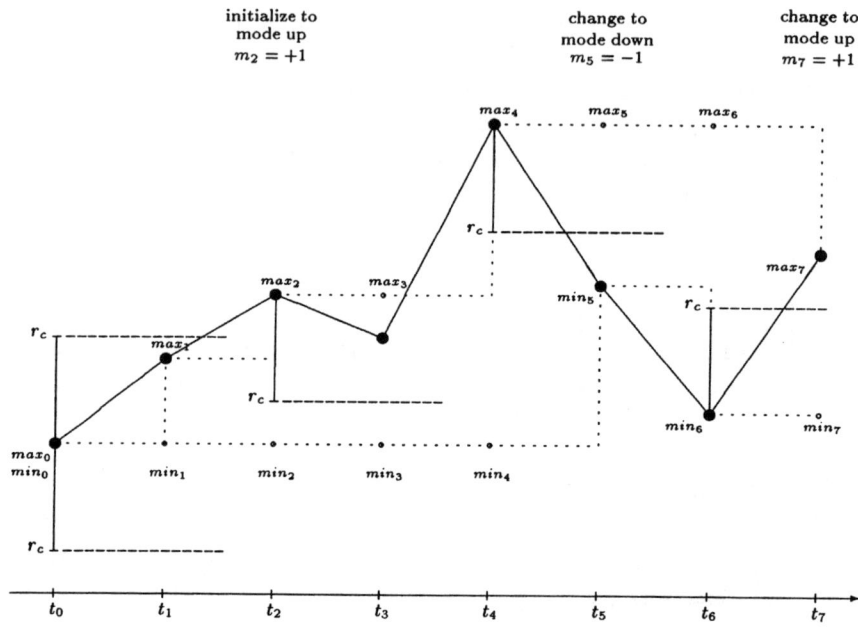

Figure 2.8: Schematic representation of the directional change algorithm

This figure described how the algorithm for the directional change frequency (see Definition 7) is implemented. The mode is only initialised to the upward mode at time t_2 since the first change at time t_1 is not significant as defined by r_c. At time t_3, the downward movement is not taken into account as it is smaller than the significance level r_c. At time t_4, we are thus still in the upward mode with the maximum value being adjusted according to the algorithm. At time t_5, the mode is reversed as the move downward is significant. At the same time, the minimum value is adjusted up to min_5. At time t_6, the minimum is again adjusted as we are still in a down mode. At time t_7, the mode is reversed to the up mode and the maximum is adjusted as the change upwards is significant. There are therefore two directional changes in total.

Chapter 3

Chaos in the Foreign Exchange Markets

In the late 80's, nonlinear dynamic systems known as deterministic chaos attracted new interest among economists (Boldrin and Woodford, 1990; Brock and Dechert, 1991; Grandmont, 1992; DeGrauwe and Dewachter, 1993). With only a few degrees of freedom – i.e. a low-dimensional[1] fractal attractor – such systems can indeed mimic a stochastic behaviour and thus reconcile the classical deterministic view with the apparent unpredictability and randomness observed in real-world data (Mirowski, 1990). These theoretical developments are promising as they provide a natural extension to traditional low-dimensional macro-economic models (see chapter 1) but have so far been limited to the analysis of the conditions of emergence of multiple and unstable equilibria. Ultimately, their empirical relevance rests on findings that detect chaotic behaviour in real-world data. Besides, the empirical investigation of chaos could reveal itself very useful for the construction of theoretical models. Indeed, empirical tests of chaos can yield some information on the structure of theoretical models such as the number of independent variables without depending on the specific functional form of the model. Moreover, they include the detection of simpler dynamics such as a unique steady state or multiple equilibria (see chapter 1). Empirical tests of chaos can thus be considered as very general tests of the adequacy of low-dimensional structural or macro-economic models.

A second and parallel source of interest for the investigation of chaos in economic time-series comes from the empirical literature on financial markets. It is by now widely accepted that financial markets are nonlinear and do not follow a simple random-walk although they seem rather unpredictable with global models (Diebold and Nason, 1990). On the other hand, the more sophisticated ARCH-like processes are not completely satisfactory as illustrated by the recent effort by Ding et al. (1993) to adapt the ARCH-model to better fit the data. The algorithms developed in the chaos literature to compute global statistics or invariants such as the fractal dimension , the spectrum of Lyapunov exponents and the Kolmogorov entropy[2] provide an interesting alternative characterisation of the financial markets. Yet again, a breakthrough of chaos in the time series literature requires convincing evidence of chaotic behaviour in the data.

A number of studies[3] have been aimed at detecting the presence of chaos in several economic time series. Regrettably, the direct application of techniques originally developed in physics presents a number of problems such as the fact that they deal with relatively short and noisy data sets as is rightly put forward in Ramsey and Yuan (1989), Ramsey et al. (1990), Ramsey and Rothman (1992). In addition to sometimes methodological problems, these are the most severe limitations of the studies mentioned above.

This chapter extends on the existing literature in that the methodology deals with the problem of noise and is applied to a very large data set consisting of both foreign exchange returns and their absolute values. We compute the fractal dimension of the foreign exchange markets, which gives a lower bound to the number of degrees of freedom of the system[4]. Furthermore, it is the first step in the empirical investigation of chaos as it provides the necessary information for the computation of the spectrum of Lyapunov exponents[5]. The methodology presented is suited to cope with reasonably small stochastic noise. In order to tackle the small sample problem, we use intradaily returns over a long period of time[6].

We also applied the algorithms on the absolute values of the exchange rates returns as a measure of the volatility to find whether the nonlinearities present in the second moment could be due to the presence of a deterministic attractor. Our main trust of findings is the absence of a low-dimensional attractor both for the foreign exchange returns and their absolute values. This questions both the practical adequacy of economic modelling based on chaos theory and the empirical relevance of the chaotic algorithms for the characterisation of the dynamics of the foreign exchange markets.

The chapter is organised as follows. In the next section, we discuss our methodology. We first present the time-delay and the singular value decomposition methods of reconstruction of the embedding phase space. We then discuss the implementation of the Grassberger-Proccacia algorithm to compute the correlation dimension . Finally, we summarise the steps to be followed. Section 3 presents our data set and results. Section 4 concludes the chapter.

3.1 Methodology

3.1.1 Reconstruction of the embedding phase space

Assume that the foreign exchange markets are described by m variables $x_0, x_1, ..., x_{m-1}$. Each variable x_k generates over time an n-vector $x_k(1), ..., x_k(n)$. Assume that the dynamics is described by the following ergodic[7] system of first order difference equations:

$$Y(t) = F(Y(t-1)), \quad t = 2, ..., n \tag{3.1}$$

where $Y(t)$ is the set $\{x_o(t), x_1(t), ..., x_{m-1}(t)\}$ and F is a smoothly differentiable nonlinear function. These m vectors span a space called phase space. Assume further that the trajectory of the system converges to an invariant subset of the phase space called attractor.

The embedding theorem (Sauer et al., 1991; Packard et al., 1980; Takens, 1981) proves that the attractor can be reconstructed without a priori knowledge of the nature of the variables or the functional form of the difference equations. The measurement in time of a single variable, say x, suffices for the characterisation of the dynamics of the system evolving in a multi-variable space.

Using the time delay method (Takens, 1981), a set of m variables can be constructed from a single time series. These variables are obtained by shifting the original time series by a fixed time lag τ, $\tau \in R^m$. We thus have the following matrix:

$$X = \{x(t), x(t+\tau), .., x(t+\tau(m-1))\}, \quad t = 1, .., n-(m-1)\tau \quad (3.2)$$

Takens proved that for $m \leq 2D + 1$ (where D is the dimension of the attractor) the phase space spanned by this set of m variables will be an embedding, i.e. it will be topologically equivalent to the original one and therefore have the same dimension and Lyapunov exponents. Unfortunately, the theorem does not specify how to determine the different parameters in eq.(3.2). First, we do not know a priori what is the dimension of the system under study. Besides, Takens does not give any indication regarding the choice of the proper time-delay τ. In practice, to avoid any spurious observation of correlation, this time-delay should correspond to the first zero of the auto-correlation function or better, to the first zero of the mutual information function (Fraser and Swinney, 1986). This respectively guarantees the linear and general independence of the subsequent elements of the matrix X but can drastically reduce the number of observations.

Another empirical problem is that for a more realistic description of the dynamics of the foreign exchange markets, equation (3.1) should be replaced by

$$Y(t) = F(Y(t-1)) + \varepsilon(t) , \quad t = 2, ..., n \quad (3.3)$$

where $\varepsilon(t)$ is a stochastic term relatively small with respect to the size of the attractor and $E[\varepsilon(t) \mid Y(t-1)] = 0$. According to eq.(3.3) the seemingly random behaviour of the foreign exchange markets is mainly due to the nonlinear self-interaction of different types of agents whose reactions can rapidly amplify the effect of any external shock or news[8]. This is in line with empirical findings on the FX markets surveyed in chapters 1 and 2. At the high-frequencies, price movements are not much influenced by external news (Goodhart, 1989). Market participants rather use the price movements to form their expectations (Takagi, 1991). At the very high frequencies, they typically trade on the basis of each other's trade (Lyons, 1997). More generally, eq.(3.3) can be seen as a very general case of low-dimensional macro-economic models (see chapter 1).

Besides economic intuition, another motivation for the use of the formulation given in eq.(3.3) is that a small noise component can result in misleading negative conclusions about the presence of a low-dimensional attractor[9].

We are however only interested in the underlying deterministic system whose dimension gives us an indication of the number of degrees of freedom of the attractor. In order to reduce the effect of small stochastic shocks without affecting the true dynamics of the system, different filters have recently been proposed[10].

A first very efficient method was suggested by Schreiber and Grassberger (1991). The phase space is first reconstructed using g delay and k advance co-ordinates. Each measurement $x(t)$ is then replaced by the average value of this co-ordinate over points in its neighbourhood in this phase space. Formally, we have

$$W = (x(t-k), ..., x(t+g)) , \quad t = k+1, ..., n-g \tag{3.4}$$

Let W_t be the t-th row $(x(t-k), ..., x(t+g))$ of the matrix W. For each W_t, let $S(W_t, \varepsilon)$ be the sphere with center W_t and radius ε, i.e.

$$S(W_t, \varepsilon) = \{W_j | d(W_t, W_j) \leq \varepsilon\} \tag{3.5}$$

where W_j is the j-th row $(x(j-k), ..., x(j+g))$ of the matrix W and the distance d is defined as follows:

$$d(W_t, W_j) \equiv \max\{|x(j-k)-x(t-k)|, ..., |x(j+g)-x(t+g)|\} \tag{3.6}$$

We then replace the present co-ordinate $x(t)$ by its mean value in $S(W_t, \varepsilon)$,

$$x(t)^{\text{corr}} = \frac{1}{|S(W_t, \varepsilon)|} \cdot \sum_{W_j \in S(W_t, \varepsilon)} x(j) \tag{3.7}$$

where $x(j)$ is the $k+1$'th co-ordinate of the vector W_j.

This local linear filter is optimal in the sense that it integrates both past and future information, i.e. along the stable and unstable directions. The phase space is then reconstructed using the time-delay method with the corrected time-series as in eq.(3.2).

An alternative way to both filter out the noise and reconstruct the attractor is based on the singular value decomposition (SVD) introduced in nonlinear dynamics by Broomhead and King (1986a, 1986b). The main idea of the SVD is to transform the embedding space into an equivalent space whose co-ordinates are linearly independent (orthogonal). Let C be the covariance matrix of the matrix X defined in eq.(3.2) (Broomhead and King, 1986a):

$$ C \ = \ X^T . X \qquad \in \ R^{mxm} \tag{3.8} $$

C is real symmetric, positive-definite and can be transformed into a diagonal matrix Λ by a series of rotations which can be expressed as:

$$ \Lambda^2 \ = \ E^T.C.E \ = \ (X.E)^T(X.E) \tag{3.9} $$

where $\Lambda^2 \ = \ \{\delta_{ij}.\lambda_i^2; i,j = 1,...,m\}$ and $E \in R^{mxm}$. The elements λ_i^2 on the diagonal of Λ^2, usually ordered by magnitude, are called eigenvalues. The vectors e_i forming the columns of the matrix E are the corresponding eigenvectors. The matrix $X.E$ represents the trajectory matrix projected onto the basis $\{e_i\}$. The choice of $\{e_i\}$ as a basis for the projection is optimal in the sense that it makes the columns of the trajectory matrix independent. This absence of correlation between the components of the trajectory matrix allows us to take a time-delay $\tau \ = \ 1$ in eq.(3.2) for the construction of $X(t)$.

Λ and E can be directly obtained from the singular value decomposition of the trajectory matrix:

$$ X \ = \ Z.\Lambda.E^T \tag{3.10} $$

where $Z \in R^{nxm}$ and $E \in R^{mxm}$ are referred to as the left and right singular vectors of X, while the elements of the diagonal matrix $\Lambda \in R^{mxm}$ are called the associated singular values.

To filter out the noise, Broomhead and King (1986a) suggest to divide the embedding space into a deterministic subspace where the orbits would stay in the absence of noise, and a stochastic subspace, in which the motion is due only to noise. They claim that from the spectrum of eigenvalues the dimension of the deterministic subspace d can be determined by identifying the eigenvalues situated above a "noise level" corresponding to a flat tail in the spectrum of eigenvalues.

Assuming that the d significant directions have been more or less correctly identified, we can split the matrix Λ as follows:

$$\Lambda = \Lambda^* + \Lambda^o \qquad (3.11)$$

where Λ^* is obtained from Λ by putting the $m - d$ eigenvalues belonging to the noise floor equal to zero, and Λ^o is also obtained from Λ by putting the d significant eigenvalues equal to zero. Replacing Λ by Λ^* or Λ^o in eq.(3.10), we obtain respectively the deterministic and stochastic components of the trajectory matrix, namely:

$$X^* = Z.\Lambda^*.E^T \quad \in \quad R^{nxm} \qquad (3.12)$$

$$X^o = Z.\Lambda^o.E^T \quad \in \quad R^{nxm} \qquad (3.13)$$

Adding eq.(3.12) and eq.(3.13), we can verify that

$$X = X^* + X^o \qquad (3.14)$$

Since we are interested in the d deterministic directions, we can project the trajectory matrix onto the deterministic subspace spanned by the eigenvectors corresponding to the eigenvalues above the noise floor as follows:

$$\underline{X} = X^*.E \quad \in \quad R^{nxd} \qquad (3.15)$$

The columns of X are often called principal components. As mentioned by Albano et al. (1988), the major drawbacks of the SVD are however the arbitrariness of the choice of both the so-called window length m in eq.(3.2) and the number of deterministic directions d. Recently, Fraedrich and Wang (1993) showed how to by-pass these problems by simply "re-embedding" the projected trajectory matrix X with the time-delay method. The re-embedding space is thus obtained as follows:

$$K = \{\underline{X}(t), \underline{X}(t+\tau), .., \underline{X}(t+\tau(m-1))\} \in R^{nx(Mxd)} \quad (3.16)$$

The topological characteristics of the re-embedding space are independent of the choice of the window-length m in eq.(3.2), the number d of deterministic directions in eq.(3.12), the re-embedding dimension M and the time-lag τ in eq.(3.16).

3.1.2 Computation of the fractal dimension

On basis of the reconstructed (re-)embedding phase space, we then compute the fractal dimension of the attractor by means of the correlation dimension algorithm proposed by Grassberger and Procaccia (1983a, 1983b). The correlation integral is defined in the M-dimensional reconstructed space as the probability of finding a pair of vectors whose distance is not larger than r :

$$C(M,r) = \frac{1}{n(n-1)} \sum_i \sum_j I\left(r - |Y(i) - Y(j)|\right) \quad (3.17)$$
$$|i - j| \geq \tau^o$$

where $I(x)$ is called the Indicator function and is valued at 1 if the distance between the two points $Y(i)$ and $Y(j)$ in the M-dimensional space is less than r, and at 0 if the distance is greater; τ^o is the correlation time due to the dynamics (Theiler, 1986). According to Grassberger and Procaccia (1983a), the correlation dimension D_2 is derived from

$$D_2 = \lim_{r \to 0} D_2(M,r) \quad (3.18)$$

for sufficiently large M, where D_2(M,r) is the slope of $C(M,r)$:

$$D_2(M,r) = \frac{d \ln C(M,r)}{d \ln(r)} \quad (3.19)$$

In other words, for r sufficiently small and for M sufficiently large, the slope of the correlation integral will saturate to the correlation dimension. In practice, one should observe a "plateau" on the plot of the correlation dimension in function of the radius r for values of M greater than m, m being an embedding in the above defined sense. We use the sup-norm as in the above nonlinear filter to compute the distance between points in eq.(4.7) and the fast box-counting algorithm proposed by Grassberger (1990). To avoid any spurious correlation estimate, the correlation time τ^o was set equal to the time-lag τ in the case of the time-delay reconstruction and to the embedding dimension m in the case of the SVD method.

A largely discussed practical problem[11] of the Grassberger-Proccacia algorithm is the minimum number of data points n_{min} needed for estimating the dimension of an attractor of dimension D. Without going into the details of the arguments, Eckmann and Ruelle (1992) suggest that

$$ n_{min} \quad > \quad 10^{(D/2)(\log(1/\rho))} \tag{3.20} $$

where $\rho = r/d \ll 1$, with r defined as above and d being the diameter of the reconstructed attractor. ρ is usually taken equal to 0.1 but can be small as 0.001 in our case. Therefore, using decimal logarithms, one easily notices that no dimension estimates higher than 2-6 can be obtained with daily data which corresponds to the estimates usually obtained[12]. This clearly points out the need for a sufficiently large data set.

3.1.3   Detection of chaos : a summary of the steps

- In order to detect the presence of low-dimension al fractal attractor, one should first check whether the *data set* has the following properties:

    - The data should be sampled at fixed time intervals. This is especially important when one computes the time predictability or entropy[13] of the system.

    - To capture fine structure, the sampling frequency should be as large as possible though not too large to avoid the problem of noise as detailed below and in chapter 2.

   – To be representative of the structure of the system, it should
     cover a sufficiently long time period, that is, at least a few
     years.

   – It should have a sufficient number of data points as derived
     in the above section.

   – Finally, the time series should be ergodic in the sense defined
     above.

Unfortunately, with the exception of the study of Mayfield and
Mizrach (1992), the data sets of the empirical studies on chaos
mentioned in the introduction do not fulfil the above conditions.
Usually, the number of data points is much too small even when
intradaily data were used (Vassilicos, 1990; Tata and Vassicilos,
1991). Moreover, even in the case of Mayfield and Mizrach, the
length of the time period covered is much too small.

• Great care should be taken in the reconstruction of the attractor.
  In particular, only Mayfield and Mizrach (1992) took care of the
  spurious auto-correlation mentioned in section (3.1.1). The noise
  should also filtered out.

• When computing the correlation integral, the correlation time (τ^o)
  in eq. 4.7 was usually not taken into account in previous studies,
  which can introduce spurious marks of a low-dimensional attractor. Besides, plots of correlation integral and correlation dimension
  estimates in function of the radius size should always be displayed.
  Then, a clear plateau should be seen on the figures of correlation
  dimension estimates. This often not the case in studies advocat-
  ing the presence of chaos such as Frank and Stengos (1989), Peters
  (1989), Blank (1991), DeCoster and Mitchell (1991).

• Finally, whenever the above methodology based on the correlation
  dimension indicates the presence of a low-dimensional attractor,
  one should be able to confirm this result by the estimation of

the dimension based on the spectrum of Lyapunov exponents as conjectured by Kaplan and Yorke (1979).

3.2 Results

3.2.1 Data

Our data set is composed of intradaily foreign exchange rates obtained from the Olsen&Associates database for the USD/DEM, GPB/USD, USD/JPY, USD/FRF[14]. The main source of this data set is the interbank spot prices published by Reuters in a multiple contributors page (the FXFX page). This covers the market world-wide and 24 hours a day. However, those prices are quotations of bid and ask prices and not actual trading prices. Furthermore, they are irregularly sampled and therefore termed as tick-by-tick prices.

In order to meet the conditions outlined in the previous section, we took equally time-spaced changes of the average of bid/ask quoted prices for a period of 6 years from the 1/1/1987 to the 12/31/1992[15]. The sampling frequency chosen are equal to 15, 30 and 60 minutes, yielding respectively approximately 294.000, 147.000 and 73.500 data points. We use the linear interpolation method to obtain price values within a data hole or any interval between ticks as in chapter 2. Outliers such as 100 times the normal price were filtered out using the low-pass filter described in the appendix of Dacorogna et al. (1993b) . We took 15 minutes as the minimum sampling interval to avoid the different possible sources of noise due to the price formation process described in chapter 2.

As in chapter 2, the intradaily returns are defined as

$$R_{idaily}(t) \quad = \quad 100[X(t) - X(t-1)] \tag{3.21}$$

where $X(t)$ is the average of the bid and ask log prices $[logP_{bid}(t) + logP_{ask}(t)]/2$ and 100 is a scaling constant so that $R_{idaily}(t)$ is expressed in percentage.

In order to avoid a too large amount of linear interpolations, we excluded the week-ends (from Friday 20.30 to Sunday 22.30 Greenwich

Mean Time) and certain holidays when all the big markets are closed. The time scale can therefore be considered as a business time scale. We argue that the choice of this time scale rather than the physical time scale does not negatively affect our results. Indeed, the omitted data points cannot be the source of the structure of the system. However, one could consider taking alternative time scales such as the de-seasonalised time (θ) proposed in Dacorogna et. (1993b).

We took the absolute values of the intradaily returns as a measure of the volatility. Although similar results can be obtained with the squared returns, the absolute values of the returns are a better measure of the volatility process as they are more significantly auto-correlated and they better reflect the seasonality of the data Taylor, 1988; Müller et al., 1990; Chapter 2). Our separate analysis of the volatility was motivated on the one hand by the existence of the second moment of the distribution (Chapter 2) and on the other hand by the non-preservability of an attractor under nonlinear transformations. In other words, the absence of a low-dimensional attractor for the returns does not imply its absence for the volatility process.

3.2.2   Results

Three different methods were used for the reconstruction of the attractor. First, we used the time-delay method described in eq.(3.2) with a time-lag τ equal to the first zero of the auto-correlation function. The same time-delay method was then applied on the filtered time series using eq.(3.4) and eq.(3.7). As suggested by Schreiber[16], we took a value of 3, 4 and 5 for the time-delay k and set it equal to time-advance g in eq.(3.4). In eq.(3.7), the size of the neighbourhood was fixed to 10 or 20 neighbours. Finally, we applied the SVD and the re-embedding technique described by eq.(3.12), eq.(3.15) and eq.(3.16). A window size m of 50 was taken as in Broomhead and King (1986a). Figures (3.1) and (3.2) show the spectrum of eigenvalues for the USD/DEM intradaily returns and their absolute values. The frequency is 1 hour. Although we do not present them here to save some place, similar figures were obtained for other frequencies and for the other currencies. It is interesting to note that the spectrum is almost flat so that no distinct noise floor can be observed on either of the two figures, with the exception of the first eigenvalue for the absolute values of the returns. This is due to the high auto-correlation observed in the volatility (Dacorogna et al., 1993). Those figures already suggest that no deterministic subspace can be distinguished. This is further confirmed by the spectrum of the first eigenvectors (figures (3.3) and (3.4)) which clearly correspond to a decomposition of the different modes of the system analogue to a Fourier decomposition. Indeed, the spectra of eigenvectors of higher order correspond to modes of higher order whereas for a chaotic process with some small stochastic noise one would notice that from some higher order on, the spectrum has a noisy shape. On the basis of those graphics, we chose a number of deterministic directions d in eq.(3.12) equal to 1 or 5 and then re-embedded the obtained manifold.

On the basis of the reconstructed attractors, we then computed the correlation integral defined in eq.(4.7) and the correlation dimension defined in eq.(3.19) as shown in figures (3.5)- (3.6) and (3.7)-(3.8) for the intradaily returns and their absolute values respectively. The reconstruction method used these figures was the SVD and re-embedding technique. Quite consistently Destexhe et al. (1988), the other two reconstruction methods – the simple time-delay and the time-delay applied on the filtered time-series – do not give different results. No distinguishable plateau or saturation of the correlation dimension can be observed on the figures for any value of the radius r. One has therefore to conclude to the absence of any clearly distinguishable low-dimensional fractal attractor in the foreign exchange markets.

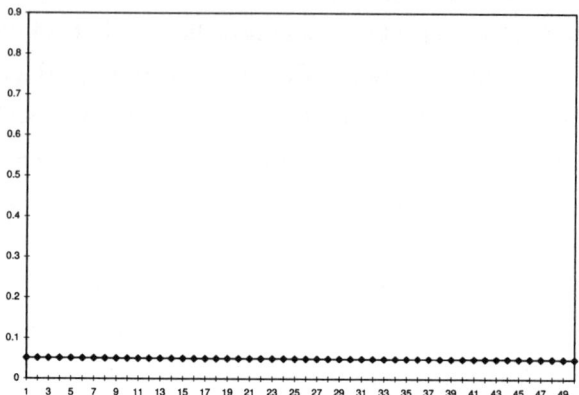

Figure 3.1: Spectrum of eigenvalues for the USD/DEM hourly price changes

Spectrum of the first 50 eigenvalues for the USD/DEM hourly price changes.

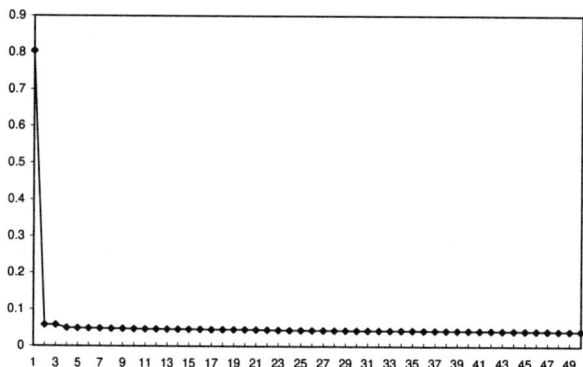

Figure 3.2: Spectrum of eigenvalues for the USD/DEM hourly absolute price changes

Spectrum of the first 50 eigenvalues for the USD/DEM hourly absolute price changes. Only the first eigenvalue corresponding to the auto-correlation can be distinguished from the flat floor of noise.

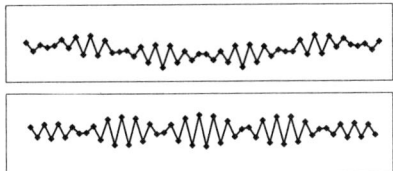

Figure 3.3: Spectrum of eigenvectors for the USD/DEM hourly price changes

Spectrum of the first 2 eigenvectors for the USD/DEM hourly price changes.

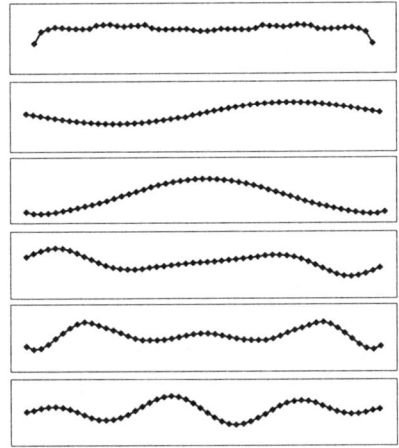

Figure 3.4: Spectrum of eigenvectors for the USD/DEM hourly absolute price changes

Spectrum of the first 6 eigenvectors for the USD/DEM hourly absolute price changes. The number of modes of the eigenvector rises with its rank, as in a Fourier decomposition.

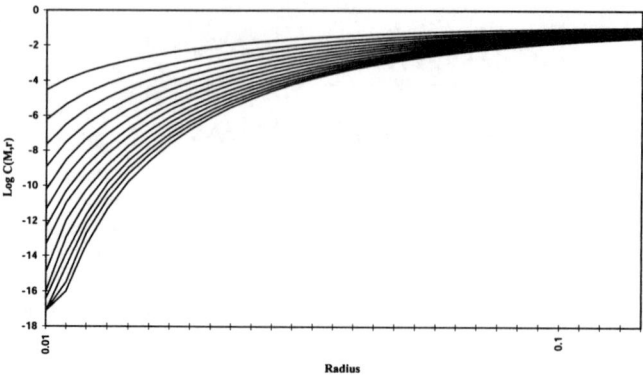

Figure 3.5: Correlation integral for the USD/DEM hourly price changes

Correlation integral for the USD/DEM hourly price changes using the singular value decomposition embedding method.

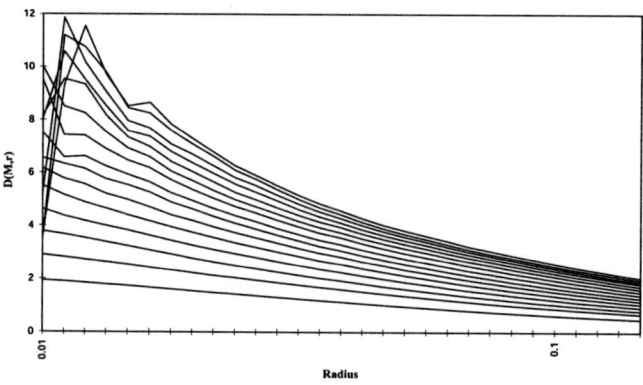

Figure 3.6: Correlation dimension for the USD/DEM hourly price changes

Correlation dimension for the USD/DEM hourly price changes using the singular value decomposition embedding method. No plateau can be observed on the figure.

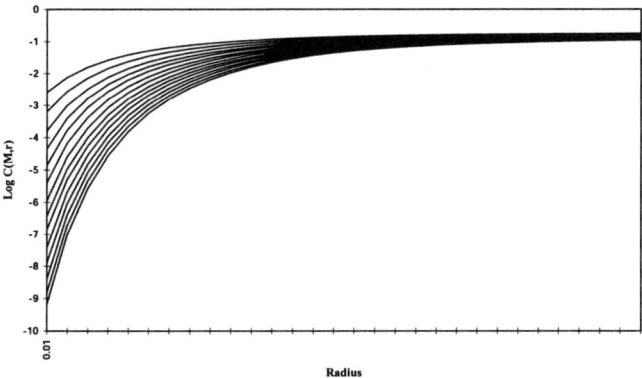

Figure 3.7: Correlation integral for the USD/DEM hourly absolute price changes

Correlation integral for the USD/DEM hourly absolute price changes using the singular value decomposition embedding method.

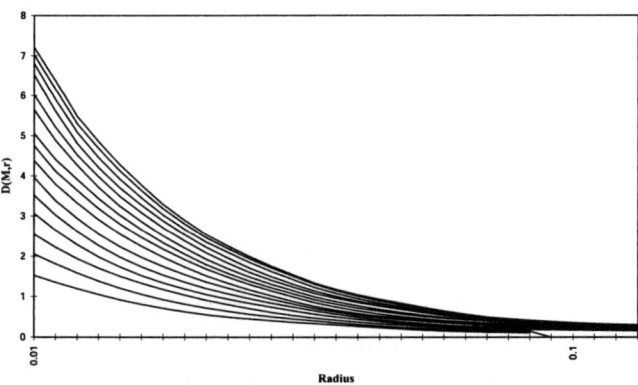

Figure 3.8: Correlation dimension for the USD/DEM hourly absolute price changes

Correlation dimension for the USD/DEM hourly absolute price changes using the singular value decomposition embedding method. No plateau can be observed on the figure.

3.3   Conclusion

In this chapter, we computed the fractal dimension of intradaily returns and of their absolute values for the main currencies against the USD using several methods for the reconstruction of the embedding phase space. A detailed implementation of the Grassberger-Proccacia algorithm for noisy data sets was presented. However, neither the application of non-linear filters nor the singular value decomposition could demonstrate the presence of a low-dimensional attractor. This is consistent with the absence of any distinguishable noise floor in the spectrum of eigenvalues.

This is further corroborated by results of dimension estimates for daily exchange rates returns for the USD/DEM, GBP/USD, USD/JPY, for the period 1973-1990, which display only mixed evidence in favour of low-dimensional fractal attractor (Dewachter and Guillaume, 1992). Indeed, on the one hand, Dewachter and Guillaume (1992) showed that these results are not completely robust to the Ramsey and Yuan (1989) procedure of correction for the small sample bias; on the other hand, the period 1973-1981, not covered by our intradaily sample, seems to be responsible for the small evidence in favour a low-dimensional fractal attractor in the case of USD/BPD. Finally, Mayfield and Mizrach (1992) found that the predictability horizon of high-frequency stock index was smaller than 15 minutes, which corresponds to our minimum time-interval.

In order to explain the absence of a low-dimensional attractor, two reasons can be put forward. First, the basic assumption underlying the application of chaos algorithms, i.e. the hypothesis of ergodicity as defined in the introduction, might not be satisfied. Unfortunately, to our knowledge, there is no formal test of ergodicity as of yet. A second reason might be that the FX markets are indeed of very high – if not infinite – dimension or complexity. This is consistent with the highly heterogeneous nature of the FX markets described in chapter 2.

However appealing these models might be from an economic point of view, our results thus question the validity of the corner-stone of low-dimensional models for FX rates, in particular of chaotic models. The only distinct feature we found so far was the auto-correlation patterns of the volatility. This strong auto-correlation of the volatility is the core of the Auto Regressive Conditional Heteroskedastic (ARCH) (Engle, 1982) class of stochastic models which will be studied in chapter 5. Another potential research path is the definition of a change of co-ordinates in the phase space such that the complexity of the system can be tackled. This change of co-ordinates could be realised either by operating a (non-)linear transformation on the foreign exchange rates or by taking a new definition of the time-scale such as in chapter 4.

Finally, the above results lead us to be very cautious with respect to results arguing the presence of a low-dimensional attractor in economic data in general. Great methodological care along the lines described in section (3.1.3) should be taken before considering dimension estimates as valid.

Footnotes

(1) We define here the number of degrees of freedom as the minimum dimension of the phase space needed to represent the system. A low-dimensional system is then defined as a system which can be embedded in R^m with $m \leq 10$. Note that systems with even an infinite range of parameters such the Mackey-Glass system can be embedded in a low-dimensional phase space. The dimension is thus a measure of degree of complexity of the structure of a system and as such, is a static measure.

(2) For good surveys of these concepts, see e.g. Eckmann and Ruelle (1985), Ruelle (1989) and Grassberger et al. (1991).

(3) (Barnett and Chen, 1988; Frank and Stengos, 1989; Eckmann et al., 1988; Peters, 1989; Scheinkman and LeBaron, 1989; Vassilicos, 1990; Ramsey and Rothman, 1992; Blank, 1991; DeCoster and Mitchell, 1991; Hsieh, 1991; Tata and Vassilicos, 1991; Dechert and Gencay, 1992; Bajo-Rubio et al., 1992; Mayfield and Mizrach, 1992; Jaditz and Sayers,

1993).

(4) See note (1) for the definition of the number of degrees of freedom. The number of degrees of freedom $\in [D, 2D + 1]$, where D is the next integer to the fractal dimension .

(5) It indicates the minimum number of "true" exponents to be computed. Note that, strictly speaking, a low-dimensional fractal attractor is not necessarily strange or chaotic and conversely (see (Eckmann and Ruelle, 1985), p.625 for a counter-example).

(6) We are grateful to B. Mizrach and C. Goodhart who respectively brought to our knowledge the existence of the paper of Mayfield and Mizrach (1992) and those of Vassilicos (1990) and Tata and Vassilicos (1991). Although those papers do not treat the problem of noise and have a data which covers a much shorter (even too short) time period, they come to similar conclusions.

(7) A system is said to be ergodic when averages in time are equal to averages in space. Therefore, an ergodic system should be autonomous or strongly stationary (for further details, see (Eckmann and Ruelle, 1985)).

(8) A similar approach to the definition of noisy chaos has been formulated by Chan and Tong (1994).

(9) Schreiber (1993) gives the example of the Mackey-Glass with 5% Gaussian noise added.

(10) Although it has not yet been formally demonstrated, simulations showed that, contrary to linear filters, these filters do not affect the dynamic of the system.

(11) See Ramsey and Yuan (1989), Smith (1988), Nerenberg and Essex (1990), Eckmann and Ruelle (1992) .

(12) As discussed in Grassberger et al. (1991) and references therein, dimensions inferior to 2 should not be mistaken as small attractor dimensions ; they rather correspond to stochastic processes.

(13) The entropy measures the rate of divergence of two nearby trajectories on the attractor as defined in Section 1 in chapter 1.

(14) Standard abbreviations of the International Organisation for

Standardisation (ISO, code 4217).

(15) See chapter 2 for a complete description of the data.

(16) Personal communication.

Chapter 4

Sources of Nonlinearities in the Foreign Exchange Markets

4.1 Introduction

Mandelbrot and Taylor (1967), Clark (1972) and Allais (1973) have introduced the concept of time deformation to model the subjective view of time held by market participants. In these models, time speeds up when the information flow rises. This information flow can be measured by the interest rate (Allais), the transaction volume (Mandelbrot and Taylor) or the volatility (Clark). These new time scales were shown to fit quite adequately the properties of the time series. Rather than the physical time, they are thus the "natural" or relevant time scale in which to measure the price generating process. More recently, Stock (1988) shows that in such time scale prices could be linearly related to the underlying fundamentals. Stock also demonstrates that this time scale could capture the conditional heteroskedasticity exhibited by the time series. With the changing volume of transactions at the intradaily frequencies, the use of such time scales seems even more relevant (Dacorogna et al., 1993b; Ghysels and Jasiak, 1994).

In this chapter, we model the structure of intradaily FX rates using two time-scale transformations. The first one is an intradaily extension of the business time scale implicitly used at daily intervals by omitting week-ends or holidays (Dacorogna et al., 1993). The second time scale (Dacorogna et al., 1996) is very similar in spirit to the time deformation models described above. Then, we identify the structure of the time series in each of these time scales using correlograms and the Brock, Dechert and Scheinkman test of independency. Our results confirm that as one raises the frequency to look at intradaily data, the nonlinearities found at the daily or weekly frequencies (see, for example, Hsieh (1989; 1991), Brock et al. (1992)) indeed increase. The stronger presence of nonlinearities is however not only due to a finer sampling through which the fatness of the tails of the distribution becomes more evident. Other sources of nonlinearites can also be identified. Finally, we show that these time-scale transformations are usefull subordinated processed for empirical micro-structure studies eventhough they cannot account for all the nonlinearites present in the data.

The remainder of this chapter is divided as follows. In the next section, we present our methodology. The third section summarises the results. The fourth section concludes the chapter.

4.2   Methodology

4.2.1   Time scale transformations

In this chapter, we use three different time scales. The first one is the physical time used in most empirical studies. In this physical time, data points are usually regularly sampled in order to create an homogeneous time series. Raw intradaily – tick-by-tick – FX quoted rates, however, arrive at an irregular pace. Therefore, we used linear interpolation over data holes such as in Müller et al. (1990) to obtain regularly spaced data in physical time.

The two other time-scales result from time-scale transformations where time is treated as a directing process like in the framework of Stock

(1988) for example. The first time process, Theta time ($\vartheta : t \to \vartheta(t)$),
models expected seasonal activity. The second time scale, intrinsic time
($\tau : \vartheta(t) \to \tau(\vartheta(t))$), models the recent activity, that is, activity over
the last hour, day or week. Unlike the models of Stock (1988) or Clark
(1972), no latent process for the FX returns is modelled in these new
time scales. Another difference is that rather than using an a priori para-
metric form like an exponential function (Stock, 1988) or a lognormal
function (Clark, 1972), we estimate the directing process in two steps
on the basis of the structural properties of the time series.

The first step in the estimation of these time scales is to estimate the
empirical scaling law relating the average volatility over a time interval
to the size of this time interval (Müller et al., 1990):

$$\overline{|r(t_i)|} = \left(\frac{\Delta t_i}{\Delta T}\right)^{1/E} \tag{4.1}$$

The drift exponent – $1/E$ – is a constant which is quite stable over the
years and across the currencies (chapter 2) and ΔT is an empirical time
constant depending upon the currency.

In a second step, we actually compute the time-scales. To get the
ϑ-time scale, we apply the inverse of the scaling law to the hourly average volatility over the whole sample period for each hour of the week
resulting in the following activity statistics:

$$a_{stat,i} \equiv \frac{\Delta T}{\Delta t}(\overline{|r(t_i)|})^{E} \tag{4.2}$$

where $\Delta t = 1$ hour and the index i refers to the hour of the week ($i = 1, ..., 168$). An activity function $a(t)$ is then fitted to the results of the
statistics $a_{stat,i}$. This activity function is divided into three components
corresponding to the three main geographical FX markets – East-Asia,
Europe and America –. Each of these markets is described by an activity
variable $a_{0,k}$ corresponding to a constant base level during the closing
hours and an activity variable $a_{1,k(t)}$ describing the activity during the
opening hours of the corresponding market (k=1, 2, 3). The ϑ-time is
then the time integral of the world-wide activity:

$$\vartheta(t) \equiv a_0 \, (t - t_0) + \sum_{k=1}^{3} \int_{t'=t_0}^{t} a_k(t') \, dt' \tag{4.3}$$

The activity variable is normalised in such a way that ϑ-time can be measured in the same units as physical time (e. g. hours, days, weeks); one full week in ϑ-time corresponds approximately to one week in physical time[1].

This ϑ-time scale thus models the deterministic seasonal patterns of the volatility caused by the geographical dispersion of market agents. Contrary to the recent model of Andersen and Bollerslev (1997), weekends, holidays and day-light saving effects are also taken into account. As shown in chapter 5, modelling these deterministic seasonal patterns through such a time scale transformation eliminates serious mis-specifications of the GARCH process as the conditional heteroskedastic structure of the data becomes more apparent.

Finally, the intrinsic time scale is used to model the remaining conditional heteroskedasticity. In this intrinsic time, the following activity variable ($a(t_j)$ where t_j refers to the unequally spaced tick-by-tick time intervals) based on the scaling law is used to model the instantaneous volatility instead of the hourly average volatility as in the ϑ-time scale:

$$a(t_j) \equiv \frac{\Delta T}{\Delta \vartheta_r}(v_r)^E \tag{4.4}$$

where v_r is the recent volatility (not annualised) and $\Delta \vartheta_r$ is a range parameter, the ϑ-time interval size of the price changes considered for computing the recent volatility v_r. In this implementation of intrinsic time, we use a more complex definition of the recent volatility than the one proposed in Dacorogna et al. (1993a), based on a sum of exponential moving averages of the volatility for different recent time horizons (Müller, 1992). The definition also takes care of the problem of holes when data are missing. The intrinsic time is then given by:

$$\Delta \tau(t_j) \equiv \frac{a(t_j)}{\overline{a}_{t_j}}\Delta \vartheta_{t_j} \tag{4.5}$$

where $\Delta \vartheta_{t_j}$ is the corresponding ϑ-time from tick to tick and $\overline{a}_{t_j}$ is the long term mean of $a(t_j)$ computed in a way that intrinsic time flows neither slower nor faster than physical time or ϑ-time in the long-term average. The underlying time scale of the intrinsic time definition is always ϑ-time rather than physical time, thus analysing the time series in its de-seasonalised form. The consequence of using such a scale is to expand periods of high volatility and contract those of low volatility, better capturing the relative importance of events to the market. To capture the temporal heterogeneity of GARCH processes (see chapter 5), we used three different time horizons for the range parameter $\Delta\vartheta_r$: 1 hour, 1 day and 1 week. Although intrinsic time incorporates the full information contained in tick-by- tick data, similarly to the ϑ time, it can easily be (temporally) aggregated. Its future flow is, however, not known and can only be obtained by a forecasting model.

4.2.2 Tests

To identify the nonlinearities present in intradaily FX rates we use correlograms of the returns and the volatility and the test for nonlinearities proposed by Brock, Dechert and Scheinkman (BDS) (1987).

The motivation for the use of *correlograms* comes from the singular value decomposition of intradaily returns and volatility performed in chapter 3 where the only distinct structure of FX rates in the spectrum of eigenvalues appeared to be the auto-correlation present in the volatility. The analysis of correlograms of the volatility given in Dacorogna et al. (1993b) indeed revealed the presence of many features of the FX market. The modelling of these patterns of the auto-correlation function of the volatility was also at the origin of the GARCH class of models that we investigated in the previous chapter.

In addition to correlograms, we use the *BDS* test which has a relatively good power against nonlinearities induced by the auto-correlation of the second moment (Lee et al., 1993). In comparison to other tests of nonlinearities like the bi-spectrum test (Hinich, 1982; Ashley et al., 1986), the BDS test offers the advantage of not depending upon the existence of higher moments. This is an important property since only the three first moments of the distribution of intradaily FX returns exist as shown in recent studies of the tail indices of these distributions (Dacorogna et al., 1994).

The BDS test is based on the following time-delay reconstruction of the phase space which is topologically equivalent to the original phase space (Takens, 1981):

$$X = \{x(t), x(t+\tau), ..., x(t+\tau(m-1))\} \quad t = 1, ..., n - (m-1)\tau \quad (4.6)$$

where x is the FX return at time t to be defined in section 4.3 and τ ($\tau \in N$) is a fixed time lag. This lag is usually taken equal to the number of lags corresponding to the first zero of the auto-correlation function to ensure linear independence of the reconstructed variables. Alternatively the time-series could be filtered by an Auto-Regressive process and then take $\tau = 1$.

Define now the correlation integral $C(m, \varepsilon)$ as follows:

$$C(m, \varepsilon) \quad = \quad \frac{1}{n(n-1)} \sum_i \sum_j \; I(\varepsilon - |X(i) - X(j)|)$$
$$i \neq j \qquad\qquad\qquad\qquad (4.7)$$

where $I(x)$ is called the Indicator Function and is valued at 1 if the distance between the two points $X(i)$ and $X(j)$ in the m-dimensional space is less than ε, and at 0 if the distance is greater. The BDS statistics is then:

$$\text{BDS} \quad = \quad n^{1/2}[C(m, \varepsilon) - C(1, \varepsilon)^m] \qquad\qquad (4.8)$$

Under the null hypothesis that the series is independently and identically distributed, the BDS is asymptotically normally distributed with zero mean and a complicated variance whose exact formulation is given in Brock et al. (1987). The parameter ε is usually taken between 0.5 and 1.5 times the standard error of the data.

4.3   Results

The basic data for this study are constructed from tick-by-tick data collected in physical time and provided by Reuters from the main FX contributors around the world, 24 hours a day, 7 days a week, for the period from the 01.01.1987 midnight Greenwich Mean Time (GMT) to the 31.12.1993 midnight (GMT). Outliers are filtered out as in (Dacorogna et al., 1993; Dacorogna et al., 1994). The variables we use are the returns

$$r(t_i) \equiv [x(t_i) - x(t_i - \Delta t)] \tag{4.9}$$

where t_i indicates a fixed sampling, with the price computed as the average of the logarithm of the bid and ask prices ($x(t_i) = [\log p_{ask}(t_i) + \log p_{bid}(t_i)]/2$). The volatility is defined as the absolute value of the returns. The FX rates are the main exchange rates against the USD: DEM, JPY, GBP, CHF and FRF.

4.3.1 The correlogram study

The major findings in Figure 4.1 concern the presence of non-deterministic seasonality in addition to deterministic seasonality of the volatility and the modelling of the high short term – ARCH type – and long term memory of the volatility by the intrinsic time scale.

From the first graph on Figure 4.1, deterministic seasonal patterns clearly appear at lags of corresponding to physical days. The second graph show that these seasonal patterns are removed by the ϑ-time scale, making the short and long term memory of the volatility more apparent. On the same graph significant waves in the autocorrelation function of the volatility together with a significant positive followed by a significant negative autocorrelation of the returns can be observed around time lags corresponding to multiples of a business day. This non-deterministic seasonality corresponds to stochastic spillovers between dealers within the same geographical market. These spillovers can hardly be attributed to the propagation of some public information like in the heat wave versus meteor shower story of Engle et al. (1990), or to some information assymetries or the openings/closings of the markets as in most micro-structure models. The only explanation to this non-deterministic seasonality we could think of, is that traders do favour the informal information regarding their own market, that is, for example, talks with one another over the phone to take the feel of the market for

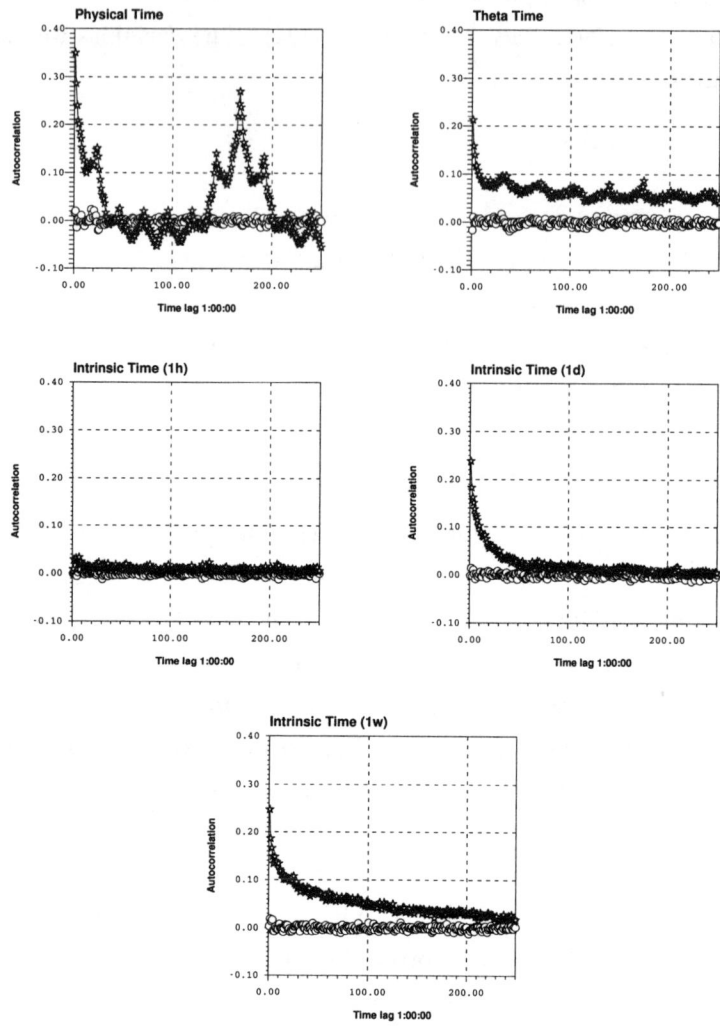

Figure 4.1: Correlograms using various time scales

The auto-correlation function for the price changes (circle) and the absolute value of the price changes (star) using different time scales: physical time, theta time, intrinsic time on 1 hour, intrinsic time on 1 day and intrinsic time on 1 week. The sampling period runs from 01.01.87 to 31.12.93. The currency is the USD/DEM.

example. As could be expected, the intrinsic time-scale which models the recent memory of the volatility eliminates the non-deterministic seasonal patterns.

Second, as could be expected, the conditional heteoskedasticity could be modelled by the intrinsic time, though not for time-horizon shorter than the one taken into consideration by the intrinsic time scale. In particular, the short and long term memory of the volatility are still present in intrinsic time at the 1 day and 1 week intervals but their effects mostly disappears at lags higher than 2 days and 2 weeks respectively. This results from the fact that the behaviour of traders at higher frequencies, in particular short term intradaily dealers, is not modelled. On the other hand, although there is still some statistically significant residual auto-correlation, the intrinsic time at 1 hour seems to capture most of the structure contained in the data. This can easily be understood as the most important segment of the market is made of intradaily short term dealers acting within the 1 hour time horizon.

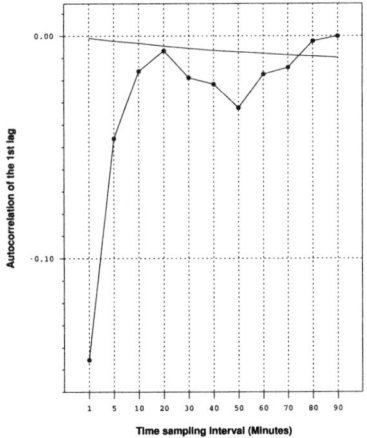

Figure 4.2: First-order auto-correlation of the DEM/USD

The sampling period runs from 01.01.87 to 31.12.93. The currency is the DEM/USD. The straight line represents the 95% confidence interval of a Gaussian random process.

Another already largely explored finding is the presence of a quantitatively negligible but statistically significant first order negative auto-correlation of the returns at the 1 hour interval can be observed both in physical and in ϑ-time. The presence of this negative auto-correlation was first reported by Goodhart (1989) on short time intervals like 1 minute and reflects the oscillation of prices quoted by dealers with diverging opinions on the price or with order imbalances (Dacorogna et al., 1993; Bollerslev and Domowitz, 1993). As can be seen from Figure 4.2, the effect of this negative auto-correlation is decreasing as one aggregates data from the 1 minute frequency to lower frequencies and becomes insignificant after 70 minutes.

4.3.2   The BDS-test results

Embedding			Sub-sample Size				
	1250	2500	5000	10000	15000	20000	Shuffled
c(2)	5.4	8.3	12.1	17.4	21.5	25.4	1.0
c(3)	6.3	9.8	14.3	20.6	25.5	31.1	1.4
c(4)	6.9	10.6	15.7	22.6	28.0	34.9	1.4
c(5)	7.4	11.5	17.1	24.4	30.4	38.8	1.4
c(6)	7.9	12.3	18.3	26.2	32.8	42.6	1.3
c(7)	8.4	13.2	19.6	28.1	35.3	46.9	1.2
c(8)	8.9	14.0	20.9	30.0	38.0	51.7	1.0
c(9)	9.5	15.0	22.4	32.1	40.9	57.0	1.1
c(10)	10.1	16.0	24.1	34.6	44.3	63.4	1.0

Table 4.1: Sample size impact on BDS results

Computation of the mean BDS results for various sub-sample sizes for the USD/DEM at the 2 hours frequency. The BDS results are the average results over the different sub-samples. The sampling period runs from 01.01.87 to 31.12.93. In the last column, the data (sample size of 20,000) were randomly re-shuffled.

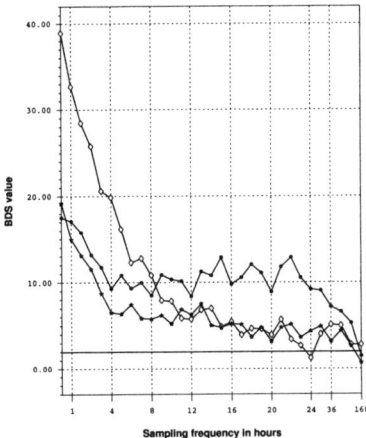

Figure 4.3: BDS results for various time scales

BDS results in function of the sampling frequency interval. The embedding dimension is 7 and the value of the radius (ε) is equal to the standard deviation. The
sampling period runs from 01.01.87 to 31.12.93. The time scales are physical time
(diamond), theta time (circle) and intrinsic time on 1 hour (star).

We first report the sensitivity of the BDS test to the size of the
sample under analysis (see also Brock et al., 1992b). In Table 4.1, the
sample size effect on the BDS results for various embedding dimension
s is shown for our particular study. A (sub-)sample size of 2500 data
points corresponds to the number of daily data contained in the whole
7 years sample. One can observe that this sample size effect is quite
important, even though the high level of nonlinearities is not simply the
result of this effect. In the last column of Table 4.1, one can see that
the presence of these nonlinearities indeed disappears when the data
are re-shuffled using a random permutation. To avoid this sample size
effect, the results that are shown in Figures 4.3 and 4.4 are the mean
BDS results for sub-samples of 2500 data points over the whole period.

The results of the BDS test for the different time scales and various
sampling frequencies are summarised in Figures 4.3 and 4.4. They are

clear evidence of the much stronger nonlinearities at the intradaily frequencies. Moreover, these results corroborate the correlogram analysis
made above in section 4.3.1.

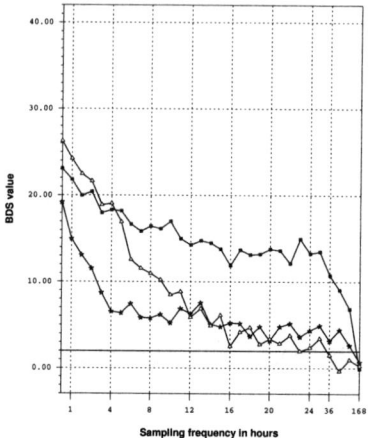

Figure 4.4: BDS results for different definitions of intrinsic time

BDS results in function of the sampling frequency interval. The embedding dimension is 7 and the value of the radius (ε) is equal to the standard deviation. The
sampling period runs from 01.01.87 to 31.12.93. The time scales are intrinsic time
on 1 hour (star), intrinsic time on 1 day (triangle) and intrinsic time on 1 week
(square).

First, the nonlinearities due to market seasonal patterns are clearly
reflected by the much higher value of the BDS in physical time for frequencies up to 8-10 hours than in ϑ-time, which approximately corresponds to the opening period of a market. However, the presence
of the non-deterministic seasonality does not appear clearly from the
BDS-analysis.

Second, the presence of short and long term memory effects is first
reflected in the ϑ-time scale for which the values of the BDS are larger for
frequencies lower than 10 hours. On the other hand, quite consistently,
values of the BDS in intrinsic time at 1 hour are much lower than in
the other time-scales. However, values of the BDS are still decreasing

for intervals up to 3-4 hours where short-term intradaily dealers are still active. Some residual structure can still be observed. On the other hand, values of the BDS in intrinsic time at 1 day and 1 week are larger up to intervals of 12 hours and 3-4 days respectively reflecting the residual short term memory not modelled by these time scales.

4.4 Conclusion

In this chapter, we have used time-subordinated processes as a simple means to model basic structural features of the intradaily FX rate time series. The main advantage of these time-scale transformations was to allow us to identify different sources of nonlinearities. Indeed, we found that the much stronger nonlinearities at the intradaily frequency do not simply result from the finer sampling of a time-series with a fat-tailed distribution. In addition to the intradaily deterministic seasonality due mainly to the geographical dispersion of traders, a non-deterministic seasonality could also be observed. This non-deterministic seasonality corresponds to higher information spillovers within a particular geographical market than across markets. Other sources of nonlinearities include the presence of short and long term memories and the price formation process taking place at the highest frequencies.

Although they could not account for all the nonlinearities present in the data, the time-scale transformations used in this chapter are a simple means to model regular patterns present not only in the volatility process but in other variables such as volume, tick frequency, spread or news. Such time-scale transformations are thus an efficient way to account simultaneously for these patterns in studies relating several of these variables. Moreover, since seasonal and conditional heteroskedastic patterns can be observed in most financial markets, these time scales could easily be transposed to other markets. In particular, they are particularly well suited to account for specific institutional features. Finally, they can easily be used in conjunction with any latent process if needed. However, one major pending issue is the integration of different time-horizons in the modelling of the memory of the volatility.

Footnotes

(1) See chapter 5 for more details on the construction of this time scale. Note that the actual normalisation is done over 4 years to include leap years and to take into account holidays effect in each market.

Chapter 5

On the Intradaily Performance of GARCH Processes

5.1 Introduction

The Auto Regressive Conditional Heteroskedastic (ARCH) model (Engle, 1982) and its Generalised version (GARCH) (Bollerslev, 1986) are now widely used in the foreign exchange literature (Bollerslev et al., 1992) and as a framework for empirical studies of the market microstructure such as the impact of news (Goodhart and Figliuoli, 1991; Goodhart et al., 1993) and government interventions (Goodhart and Hesse, 1993; Peiers, 1997), or inter- and intra-market relationships (Engle et al., 1990; Baillie and Bollerslev, 1990). A main assumption behind this class of models is the relative homogeneity of the price discovery process among market participants at the origin of the volatility process. In other words, the conditional density of one GARCH process can adequately capture the information content of news. In particular, GARCH parameters for the weekly frequency theoretically derived from daily empirical estimates are usually within the confidence interval of weekly empirical estimates (Drost and Nijman, 1993).

However, several empirical evidences seem at odds with this homogeneous view of the market. First, the long memory of the volatility (Dacorogna et al., 1993; Ding et al., 1993) indicates the presence of several market components corresponding to several time-horizons (see Baillie et al. (1993) for an extended GARCH model that incorporates this long memory). Even so, empirical results on the temporal aggregation of a (mis-specified) GARCH process with daily data where the long memory property can be observed, are consistent with the prediction of the theory (Drost and Nijman, 1993). Second, at the intradaily frequency, round-the-clock time series reveal seasonal patterns that reflect, among others, the geographical dispersion of the traders, concentrated in three main geographical areas, Asia, Europe and America. Third, exchange rates movements are not necessarily related to the arrival of news when looked at the intradaily frequency (Goodhart, 1989), reflecting the fact that intra-day traders may have other constraints and objectives than, for example, longer term traders. Fourth, at the extremely high frequencies, FX rates exhibit distinct characteristics due to the price formation process (see Chapter 2).

In this chapter, we investigate the importance of these different sources of heterogeneity for the modelling of the FX markets using the GARCH setting. More specifically, we show that estimates of a GARCH process with data in physical time are likely to be spurious, even though estimates for one particular frequency seem to be reasonable. Estimates are only consistent across currencies when the seasonal patterns are fully taken into account. However, even when these seasonal patterns are accounted for, the aggregation properties of the GARCH model break down at the intradaily frequencies. One can also observe the effects of the price formation process at frequencies higher than the 1 1/2 hour time interval. Finally, the instability of coefficient estimates over different sub-periods of 6 months suggests the presence of – possibly random – structural changes in the volatility process in the very long run.

The remainder of this chapter is divided as follows. In section 5.2, we present the data and describe regular patterns such as the seasonal deterministic components and its fractal structure. A different time scale which integrates these patterns is discussed in section 5.3. In section 6.3, we present results of GARCH estimates for several frequencies in both physical time and de-seasonalised time. Section 6.4 concludes the chapter.

5.2 Description of the data

As in previous chapters, in this chapter we use a 7-years data bank of intradaily foreign exhange quotes for the period from 1.01.1987 to 31.12.1993 for the major currencies against the USD, that is the DEM, JPY, GBP, FRF and CHF. As in Müller et al. (1990) and Dacorogna et al. (1993), linear interpolation over time is used to determine price values within data holes and to generate regularly spaced time series. A minimum time interval of 10 minutes was taken to avoid price uncertainty (see chapter 2). Price are computed as the average of the logarithm of the bid and ask prices ($x(t_i) = [\log p_{bid}(t_i) + \log p_{ask}(t_i)] / 2$ where t_i indicates a fixed sampling) and returns as the corresponding price changes ($r(t_i) = [x(t_i) - x(t_i - \Delta t)]$). Table 2.4 in the Appendix of Chapter 2 gives a summary of the properties of these time series for the main intervals as well as the weekly frequency. One very apparent feature of this table is the very fast increase of the kurtosis of the returns with increasing sampling frequency. This major characteristic of FX returns is the direct consequence of the non-convergence of the fourth moment of the distribution (see Dacorogna et al., 1997). This already suggests that in modelling the conditional heteroskedasticity, it might be more adequate to use (non-integer) powers of the absolute value of the returns smaller than two as in the GARCH model (Ding et al., 1993).

A second characteristic of intradaily returns is the strong seasonal deterministic structure of the intradaily volatility (see chapter 2). The presence (or absence) of the different geographical markets can easily be seen in the autocorrelation patterns, with much stronger auto-

correlation patterns at lags that are integer multiples of seasonal patterns. Although several studies of the micro-structure of the market
have already tried to establish a causal link between these different geographical markets and the conditional heteroskedasticity of the returns,
they did not make the distinction between conditional and seasonal heteroskedasticity in their empirical models. One reason for this short-
coming of previous studies is that they concentrate their analysis on
data at one particular frequency. As will be demonstrated in section 6.3,
one can easily overlook this deterministic seasonal feature as empirical
estimations for one particular frequency may appear reasonable.

A third characteristic of intradaily returns of interest for our study
is their fractal structure in the sense of Mandelbrot (1983); that is, the
average FX rate volatility measured over a time interval is linked to the
size of the interval by a power law. Note that the different statistical
properties at different frequencies of FX rates imply that FX rates are
neither self-similar fractals nor fractional brownian motions. Formally,
we have (Müller et al., 1990):

$$\overline{|r(t_i)|} \quad = \quad \left(\frac{\Delta t_i}{\Delta T}\right)^{1/E} \tag{5.1}$$

where $\overline{|r(t_i)|}$ is the absolute value of the average return, Δt_i is the time
interval over which the return is computed, ΔT is a regression constant
which depends upon the FX rates and $1/E$ is the drift exponent. In
estimating equation 5.1, the lowest time interval is 10 minutes and the
largest 2 months, which yields an aggregation ratio of more than 8750.
Taking the logarithm on both sides, one can estimate the drift exponent
$- 1/E$ – by ordinary least squares. The computation of the standard
errors takes into account both the uncertainty due to the relative size
of the spread and the uncertainty due to the sample size. The drift
exponent is a constant with a value of around 0.6 which is quite stable
over the years and across the currencies (Chapter 2). This is remarkable
since for all statistical distributions typically referred to in studies of FX
markets such as the Gaussian, the Student-T with 3 degrees of freedom,
the Cauchy and a theoretical GARCH process, empirical simulations

with a similar aggregation ratio yield a value of the drift exponent of about 0.5.

In the above relationship the absolute value of the returns was taken as a measure of the volatility but the same relationship is valid for their squared value. Thus, notwithstanding the changing empirical distributions for different frequencies, this relationship provides a way to relate the average volatility at the various frequencies. This empirical law will be used in the next section to model the deterministic seasonal pattern of the volatility.

A fourth characteristic of intradaily returns is the price formation process which takes place at the highest frequencies (Chapter 2) 1997). In particular, the high short term negative auto-correlation makes the nonlinear structure of FX rates even more complex (Chapter 4). Moreover, the size of the spread is comparable to the size of price changes to frequencies up to 80 minutes.

5.3 Alternative time scales

As noted in earlier chapters, the definition of the adequate time-scale is not as straightforward as it could appear at first sight. When we described intradaily data, we already implicitly discussed two different time scales in the case of intradaily data: regularly and irregularly – tick by tick – spaced prices. To avoid uncertainty on the price, we took a minimum time interval of 10 minutes to compute returns in physical time. Observations during week-end are, however, rather sparse, causing an abrupt change in the shape of the auto-correlation function of the volatility. A crude way to treat this problem is the definition of a business time scale in the same way as it is usually done with daily observations by simply omitting observations corresponding to the week-ends when the markets are virtually closed,– that is, in our case, from Friday 22.30 GMT to Sunday 22.30 GMT –. In the remainder of this chapter, we will refer to this time scale without the week-end observations as the business time scale.

As discussed in the previous section, one of the characteristics of very high frequency FX rates is their intradaily seasonality. One option to account for this intradaily seasonality chosen by and Bollerslev (1996) is to use the previously defined business time scale and fit a flexible Fourier form such as in Gallant (1981) to the average intradaily volatility over 5-minutes time periods. Although their model originally has a very large number of parameters, empirical estimations eventually allow them to reduce it to the more parsimonious number of 14. They also seem to obtain a reasonably fit of the intradaily seasonal pattern. However, the major drawback of their approach is that it does not differentiate between the different geographical markets present in the FX – namely, Asia, Europe and America –, nor does it incorporate available information on Day Light Saving Time or holidays such as the Emperor day in Japan.

As shown in Chapter 2, seasonality patterns correspond to the presence or activity of market participants. Average volatility, quote frequency and, although it is usually not observed in the FX markets, supposedly volume, are higher when different geographical markets are simultaneously opened and dropped during lunch time hours in Europe or Japan and week-ends. No micro-structure theory has of yet successfully accounted for this phenomenon in the FX markets (see, for example, the discussion in Hsieh and Kleidon (1996)), but there is substantial empirical evidence on the contemporaneous relation between these statistics (see, for example, Lamoureux and Lastrapes (1990)). To fully account for the seasonal patterns, one should therefore incorporate all the available information on the presence of the main markets in a model of market activity. In this chapter, we follow Dacorogna et al. (1993) who, in a similar way to Allais (1966), Mandelbrot and Taylor (1967), Stock (1988) and Ghysels and Jasiak (1994), model market activity by introducing a different time scale as the directing process theta ($\vartheta(t)$) of the subordinated price generating process $x(t) = x^*[\vartheta(t)]$, where the process x^* is de-seasonalised. In addition to incorporating existing information on the markets to model the seasonal patterns, the main advantage of using this new time scale is that it allows time aggregation, one of the objective of this chapter. In the remainder of this section, we describe in some more details this time scale.

The time scale $\vartheta(t)$ is a strictly monotonic function of physical time t, which is constructed by defining an activity variable a as the ratio of the interval sizes on the different scales

$$a_{1,2} \equiv \frac{\vartheta_2 - \vartheta_1}{t_2 - t_1} \tag{5.2}$$

This activity variable reflects the seasonal volatility patterns. It is computed in two steps.

First, we define *activity statistics* $a_{stat,i}$ with the help of the empirical scaling law of price changes given in equation 5.1. Taking $t_2 - t_1$ equivalent to one hour and applying the inverse of the scaling law on the average hourly volatility for each hour of the week ($\overline{|r(t_i)|}, i = 1, ..., 168$), we have that the activity of the ith hourly subsample directly follows from equation 5.2

$$a_{stat,i} = \frac{\Delta T}{\Delta t} (\overline{|r(t_i)|})^{\mathrm{E}} \tag{5.3}$$

where $\Delta t = 1$ hour.

In a second step, we define the *activity function* $a(t)$ as the sum of the three main geographical components of the FX markets (America, East-Asia and Europe):

$$a(t) \equiv \sum_{k=1}^{3} a_k(t) \tag{5.4}$$

This total activity should model the intra-weekly pattern of the statistical activity $a_{stat,i}$ as close as possible. For each market, we define the activity (a_k) as the sum of a small constant base level describing the activity during closing hours such as week-ends or holidays ($a_{0,k}$) and a much stronger, varying, positive activity ($a_{1,k}$). The activity during opening hours, $a_{1,k}$, is modelled with a polynomial with smooth transition to the constant behaviour of the closing hours. This choice is arbitrary but mathematically convenient since such functions are easily differentiable and analytically integrable. The number of free parameters of this polynomial is just sufficient to model the smooth transitions, the lunch break found in the quote frequency statistics, and a certain skewness (the relative weights of morning and afternoon). Formally, we have:

$$a_{1,k}(t_i) \equiv \begin{cases} o & \text{if } T_k < o_k \quad \text{or} \quad T_k > c_k \quad \text{or weekend} \\ a_{open,k}(t_i) & \text{if} \quad o_k < T_k < c_k \quad \text{and not week-end} \end{cases} \quad (5.5)$$

where o_k and c_k are respectively the opening and closing hours which can be approximated by the quote frequency statistics; T_k is essentially GMT time defined for technical convenience as $T_k \equiv [(t_i + \Delta t_k) \text{modulo}(24 \text{ hours})] - \Delta t_k$ with Δt_k having a value of 9 hours for East Asia, 0 for Europe, and -5 hours for America; the week-end condition $((t_i + \Delta t_k) \text{modulo}(168 \text{ hours}) \geq 120 \text{ hours})$ depends on the market; and, $a_{open,k}(t_i)$ is defined by

$$a_{open,k}(t_i) \equiv \frac{\omega_k}{\frac{o_k+c_k}{2} - s_k}(T_k - o_k)^2(T_k - c_k)^2(T_k - s_k)[(T_k - m_k)^2 + d_k^2] (5.6)$$

where ω_k represents the scale factor of the kth market, s_k the skewness of the activity curve, m_k the place of the relative minimum around the noon break, and d_k determines the depth of this minimum. This model applies to all markets. But, in the case of the America, the parameter d_3 diverges as a result of the missing noon break in this market. Equation 5.6 for America thus degenerates to a simpler form with no local activity minimum:

$$a_{open,3}(t_i) \quad \equiv \quad \frac{\omega_3}{\frac{o_3+c_3}{2} - s_3}(T_3 - o_3)^2(T_3 - c_3)^2(T_3 - s_3) \quad (5.7)$$

The model is completed by the following constraints on the parameters: to ensure positive activities, a_0 and ω_k must be positive and s_k outside the opening hours, whereas the parameter m_k should be within the opening hours as it models noon break.

The funtions $a_{1,k}(t_i)$ are then fitted to the hourly series $a_{stat}(i)$ from equation 5.3 by minimizing the sum over the intra-weekly sample of the weighted square deviation of $a(t_i)$ from $a_{stat}(i)$. To account for the Day Light Saving observed in Europe and America, we convert the time constants in equations 5.6 and 5.7 from GMT to a typical local time scale of the market. This conversion yields different results for the local times in summer and in winter. Given the sample used in the activity fitting is composed of approximately half summer and half winter, we chose to fix the time constants to the mean of the summer and winter conversion results. The computation of the activity function and the ϑ-time is then based on equation 5.5 with these local time constants.

Finally, to measure the quality of the ϑ time scale, we compute the ratio of the volatility fluctuation during the week measured in ϑ-time to the volatility fluctuation in physical time, where the volatility fluctuation is defined as the RMS value of $|\overline{r(t_i)}|$ around the mean,

$$F_{v(t)} = \left[\frac{1}{168} \sum_{i=1}^{168} \left(|\overline{r(t_i)}| - \frac{1}{168} \sum_{i=1}^{168} |\overline{r(t_i)}| \right)^2 \right]^{1/2} \tag{5.8}$$

The value of the ratio $F_{v(\vartheta)}/F_{v(t)}$ is equal to 1 for the physical time and should tend to 0 for a perfect fit of the ϑ-time scale. In our case, values between 0.25 and 0.29 were obtained for all rates. Similar results were found when the activity function was fitted to 20-minutes activity statistics instead of hourly ones.

5.4 Results

In order to test the effects of the geographical and temporal heterogeneity of the markets, we used the Likelihood procedure to fit the simple following GARCH(1,1) on the time series for several frequencies and time scales:

$$h(t) = \alpha_0 + \alpha_1.\varepsilon^2(t-1) + \beta_1.h(t-1) \tag{5.9}$$

where $h(t)$ is the conditional variance and $\varepsilon^2(t)$ is the squared innovation. At the highest frequencies (less than 2 hours), we included a MA(1) term in the mean equation to account for the statistically significant auto-correlation of the returns at these frequencies.

The algorithm used for the numerical optimisation of the Likelihood is a multi-steps iterative procedure that combines a Genetic Algorithm

(GA) with the Berndt, Hall, Hall and Hausman (BHHH) algorithm (Berndt et al., 1974). In this algorithm the number of iterations is fixed. For the first iteration, the GA initialises a fixed number of potential solutions for the parameters (Goldberg, 1989). These solutions might either be chosen randomly or be picked up from a given set of initial solutions (for example, solutions for similar problems). In this chapter, we chose the random initialisation to avoid any a priori bias in the estimation.

At each iteration, the Likelihood function is evaluated for each potential solution. Then the best solution is used as an initial solution for the BHHH algorithm. The solution obtained with the BHHH algorithm is added to the set of potential solutions for the next iteration. At each new iteration the major part of the population of solutions is replaced by some modified solutions. Only a limited number of the best individuals (5-10%), including the solution obtained with the BHHH algorithm, are kept unchanged. We also eliminate all duplicate solutions to maintain population diversity. The selection of solutions for reproduction (parents) is proportional to their Likelihood value. The new potential solutions (children) are obtained through *cross-overs* and *mutation*. In the cross-over, the corresponding parameters of the two parents are exchanged or replaced by interpolated values[1]. In the mutation, some parameter values are randomly selected into a specific range. Of course, there is an infinite set of possible mutations. Mutations are therefore much less used than cross-overs – 5% and 80-90% respectively – but they allow to occasionally yield a new random starting point.

The specific number of potential solutions per generation is somewhat arbitrary and depends on the following compromise: the higher the number of potential solutions, the longer the computation time for each generation but the smaller the number of generations needed to obtain convergence. For practical purposes, convergence is reached when the optimal solution for a specified generation remains unchanged in the next few generations, where it usually sufficient to define few as 5 to 10 generations. In this chapter, we use 100 generations of 100 individuals.

Total convergence was however usually achieved after 10 generations.

The main advantage of this method is to avoid to be trapped in local minima with the BHHH algorithm, as the set of potential solutions for the next generation of the GA includes randomly chosen solutions. This is especially important given the potential (and observed) complex dynamics of intradaily FX rates volatility. The method is also very fast, notwithstanding the very large number of observations (368.000 data points for the 10 minutes frequency). At the end, robust standard errors were computed using White's variance-covariance matrix (White, 1980).

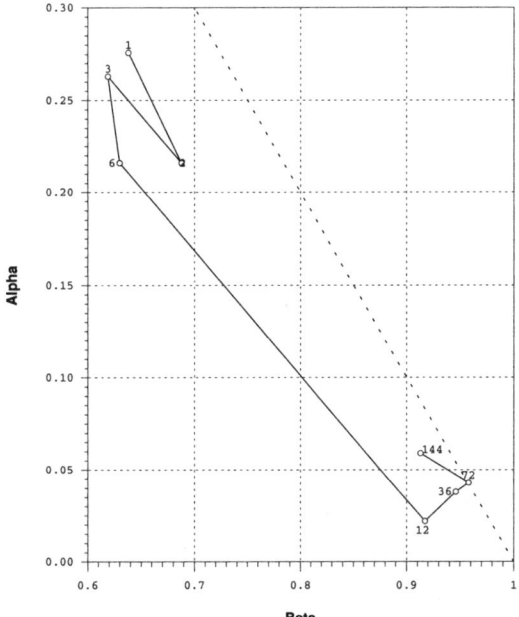

Figure 5.1: Aggregation of the GARCH(1,1) coefficients in business time.

Aggregation of the GARCH(1,1) for estimated coefficients in business time for the USD/FRF for different aggregation factors (1 = 10 m; 2 = 20 m; 3 = 30 m; 6 = 1 h; 12 = 2 h; 36 = 6 h; 72 = 12 h; 144= 24 h). The diagonal dotted line represents the limit for which $\alpha + \beta = 1$.

5.4.1   Impact of the seasonal heterogeneity

As could be expected, the use of the physical time scale caused a complete break-down of the estimation procedure yielding α_1 estimates in equation 9 as large as 4.0. This is, of course, due to the presence of the week-ends where massive linear interpolations are made. In these periods where the computed returns are usually equal to zero, it is indeed difficult to optimise a non-linear function such as the Likelihood function for the GARCH model.

We then re-estimated the model in the previously defined business time scale. The circles in Figure 5.1 correspond to the estimation of the α_1 and β_1 coefficients for the USD/FRF for several frequencies. Although the coefficient estimates may look quite reasonable at one particular frequency, the global picture for all the frequencies appears quite odd. In particular, the coefficient estimates for frequencies higher than the 2 hours time interval reflect the much more complex behaviour of FX returns at these frequencies (Chapter 4). Moreover, for certain currencies, the sum of the coefficients α_1 and β_1 can exceed unity. The latter is in line with the estimation of several micro-structure studies done so far (see also, for example, the estimated coefficients in Goodhart et al. (1993, Table I)).

Therefore, once again, we re-estimated the model using the ϑ-time scale to account for the geographical heterogeneity of the markets. The results for the USD/DEM are represented in Figure 5.2 by circles. More detailed results for each currency can also be found in Tables 5.1 to 5.3 in the Appendix. This time, contrary to results in business time, coefficient estimates are quite similar across FX rates and reasonably homogeneous from one frequency to another. This indicates the importance of accounting for this seasonality in micro-structure empirical studies of the FX markets. In particular, this is true for the investigation of the impact of news using news items from Reuters' screens such as in Goodhart et al. (1993). The analysis of lead-lag relations between different markets (Engle et al., 1990; Baillie and Bollerslev, 1990) should clearly also make the distinction between deterministic seasonality and conditional heteroskedasticity.

However, even when the deterministic seasonality is modelled, this does not imply that the GARCH model describes the volatility process at the intradaily frequencies as adequately as it seems to do at the daily or weekly frequencies. One easy test is to check whether the temporal aggregation properties of the GARCH model hold at the intradaily frequencies.

Thus, even when one takes into account the impact of the seasonality, the information content of the conditional density is not the same for different frequencies. This could be due to different volatility processes being relevant at different frequencies. Müller et al. (1997) presents an extension of the ARCH model which explicitly takes into account the presence of different volatility processes.

5.4.2 Impact of the temporal heterogeneity

The GARCH model can be viewed as describing either a jump process (Drost and Nijman, 1993) or a diffusion process (Nelson, 1990). In both cases, the sum of the α_1 and β_1 in equation 9 should tend to 1 with β_1 tending to 1 and α_1 tending to 0, as the frequency becomes higher and higher. In other words, the higher the frequency, the greater the number of periods during which the effect of shocks on the volatility will last. The Nelson (1990) results hold under very general conditions, even when the GARCH process is mis-specified, provided that no deterministic seasonal effects are present. In Figure 5.2, the coefficients α_1 and β_1 in equation 9 derived theoretically from the formula of Nelson (1990) are represented by triangles[2]. The theoretical coefficients were computed on the basis of the daily estimated coefficients. Our choice was motivated by the empirical validation of theoretical results starting from the daily frequency. Another reason for disaggregating rather than aggregating the theoretical coefficients, is the presence of additional features such as significant autocorrelation patterns complexifying the volatility dynamics at the highest frequencies (10 minutes).

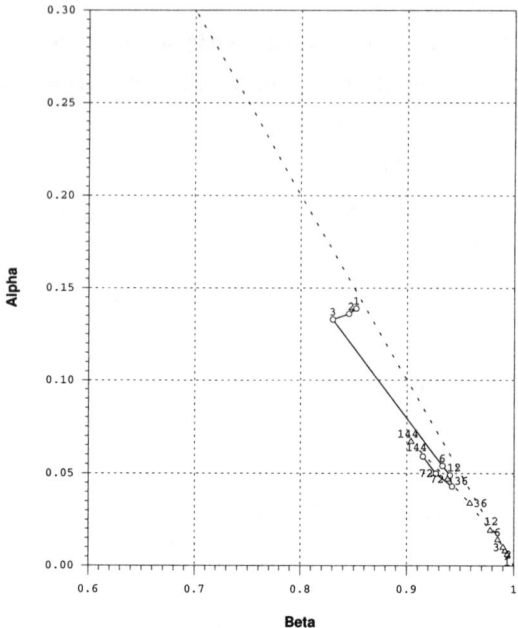

Figure 5.2: Aggregation of the GARCH(1,1) coefficients in Theta-time.

Aggregation of the GARCH(1,1) for estimated coefficients in ϑ-time (o) and theoretically derived coefficients ($\triangle$) using the Nelson results for the USD/DEM for different aggregation factors (1 = 10 m; 2 = 20 m; 3 = 30 m; 6 = 1 h; 12 = 2 h; 36 = 6 h; 72 = 12 h; 144= 24 h). The diagonal dotted line represents the limit for which $\alpha + \beta = 1$.

As can be checked in Tables 5.1 until 5.3 in the Appendix, although the coefficient estimates in the case of the ϑ-time scale seem quite reasonable, they are outside the significance interval of the coefficients that are derived theoretically. Moreover, the α_1's increase slowly whereas the β_1's decrease and the sum of the two parameters does not really tend to 1 as one goes from the daily to higher frequencies. Besides, at frequencies higher than 2 hours, the sum of the two parameters start to decrease, implying even less volatility persistence. As already noted in the case of the business time scale, this reflects the much more complex behaviour of FX returns at these frequencies. This probably also explains that no convergence of the algorithm was obtained at these frequencies for the maximisation of the likelihood function of the GARCH model using a T-Student distribution instead of the normal distribution such as in Baillie and Bollerslev (1989).

5.4.3 Stability across the sample period

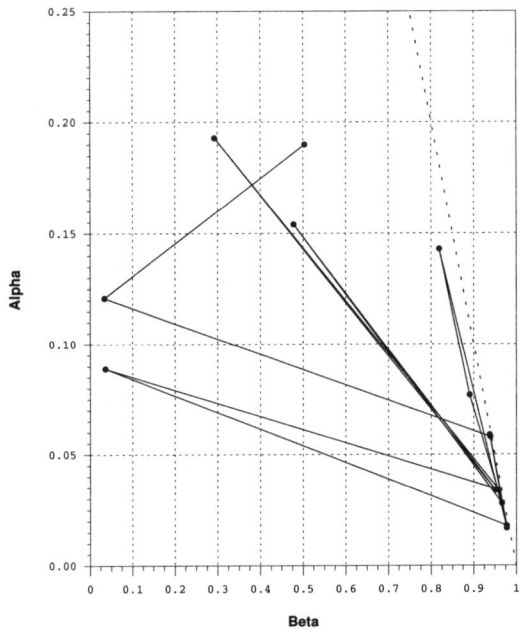

Figure 5.3: Temporal stability of the GARCH(1,1) coefficient estimates.

The temporal stability of the GARCH(1,1) coefficients for sub-periods of six months for the USD/DEM at the 2 hours frequency. The time scale is the ϑ-time. The diagonal dotted line represents the limit for which $\alpha + \beta = 1$.

There is a priori no reason why the persistence of the volatility should be constant over time. Structural breaks could result from evolving market structures or changing views on the relevant underlying fundamentals. Therefore, we looked at the temporal stability of the coefficient estimates for several sub-samples. Figure 5.3 gives the estimations of the GARCH parameters for the USD/DEM at the 2 hours time-interval, for sub-samples of six months, yielding 2,190 observations per sub-sample in ϑ-time. As can be seen, the coefficients are not stable over time. For example, whereas α_1 and β_1 are equal to 0.059 and 0.938 respectively for the first 6-months period and to 0.017 and 0.978 respectively for the second 6-months period, α_1 and β_1 for the first year are equal to 0.338 and 0.698 respectively. The estimation of the Quasi-Likelihood Ratio test of the equality of the parameters across the sub-samples yields a value of 273 compared to the corresponding critical value of 29.8 at the 0.005 level. We performed the same exercise with sub-samples of three months at the 10 minutes frequency and obtained an even much larger value of 7.300 for the Quasi-Likelihood Ratio compared to the corresponding critical value of 55.5. Moreover, the absence of dynamic pattern in the evolution of the α_1's and β_1's reflects seemingly random changes in the dynamics of the volatility process of FX rates. Our results are thus consistent with the observed random changes of fundamentals in the relatively long run. Modelling of the volatility along the avenue of the Switching-GARCH model of Gray (1996) for example, would allow further investigation on the sources of these shifts.

5.5   Conclusion

In this chapter, we assessed the impact of the heterogeneous behaviour of the FX markets on the intradaily performance of the GARCH model. We found that the various sources of deterministic seasonality present in intradaily returns introduced severe mis-specifications in the estimation of a GARCH(1,1) process. These mis-specifications invalidate the results of previous empirical micro-structure studies using the GARCH framework. We also showed that these inefficiencies could best be dealt with by the use of a time-scale transformation. But, even in this new time-scale, the aggregation properties of the GARCH break down at the intradaily frequencies, revealing the presence of at least two components corresponding to different time-horizons. The challenge of explicitly modelling these different time-components will be an important issue in future research. Some first attempts of tackling this problem in the framework of the ARCH approach can been found in Müller et al. (1997) and also in Andersen and Bollerslev (1997).

Furthermore, we identified the presence of very long-term, seemingly random, changes in the volatility dynamics. These long-term changes in the volatility dynamics are consistent with the observed changes of view on the relevant underlying fundamentals in the long run. Modelling of the volatility along the avenue of, for example, the switching-GARCH model of Gray (1996), would allow further investigation on the sources of these shifts.

Finally, we could also detect distinct patterns at frequencies higher than 2 hours. In particular, the effects of the price formation process taking place at the 10 minutes frequency were found to cause a lower persistence of the volatility.

Footnotes

(1) For example, define two solutions as the following vectors $\{\alpha_{0,1,p},$ $\alpha_{1,1,p},\ \beta_{1,1,p}\}$ and $\{\alpha_{0,2,p},\ \alpha_{1,2,p},\ \beta_{1,2,p}\}$; then the new solutions obtained by cross-overs could be defined as $\{\alpha_{0,1,c},\ \alpha_{1,1,c},\ \beta_{1,1,c}\} = \{\alpha_{0,1,p} + m.(\alpha_{0,2,p} - \alpha_{0,1,p}),\ \alpha_{1,1,p},\ \beta_{1,1,p}\}$ and $\{\alpha_{0,2,c},\ \alpha_{1,2,c},\ \beta_{1,2,c}\} = \{\alpha_{0,1,p} + (1 - m).(\alpha_{0,2,p} - \alpha_{0,1,p}),\ \alpha_{1,2,p},\ \beta_{1,2,p}\}$ respectively, where m is a constant $(= 0.33$ or $0.4)$.

(2) Similar results were obtained using the Drost and Nijman (1993) formula. Conditions to apply the Drost and Nijman formula are however more difficult to meet: from the following condition on the estimated coefficients α_1 and β_1 in equation 9: $3\alpha_1^2 + 2\alpha_1\beta_1 + \beta_1^2 < 1$ (see Bollerslev (1986), p. 312), the existence of the fourth moment of the distribution can be checked to hold for all the currencies for most

frequencies except the 10 minutes time-interval where other dynamical patterns are present. But, among others, the long term dependancy apparent in the autocorrelation function of the volatility implies that a GARCH(1,1) is mis-specified and the true underlying process (in the ϑ time scale) cannot any longer be considered as a weak GARCH process. One could however argue that this is also the case for data at daily or weekly frequencies for which the formulas hold empirically.

5.6 Appendix

rate	freq.	M.L.	α_0	α_1	β_1	$\alpha_1 + \beta_1$	α_1'	β_1'	$\alpha_1' + \beta_1'$
USD/DEM	10 m	-0.61076	$0.57 \cdot 10^{-6}$ $(0.61 \cdot 10^{-7})$	0.138 (0.0092)	0.858 (0.0080)	0.996	0.005	0.995	1.000
	20 m	-0.97428	$0.29 \cdot 10^{-5}$ $(0.12 \cdot 10^{-5})$	0.164 (0.0266)	0.788 (0.0536)	0.952	0.007	0.993	1.000
	30 m	-1.19167	$0.35 \cdot 10^{-5}$ $(0.94 \cdot 10^{-6})$	0.125 (0.0225)	0.840 (0.0286)	0.965	0.009	0.991	1.000
	1 h	-1.54224	$0.18 \cdot 10^{-5}$ $(0.14 \cdot 10^{-5})$	0.044 (0.0190)	0.945 (0.0277)	0.989	0.012	0.987	0.999
	2 h	-1.89236	$0.41 \cdot 10^{-4}$ $(0.18 \cdot 10^{-5})$	0.049 (0.0016)	0.940 (0.0017)	0.989	0.017	0.980	0.997
	6 h	-2.44953	$0.14 \cdot 10^{-3}$ $(0.16 \cdot 10^{-4})$	0.043 (0.0033)	0.942 (0.0041)	0.985	0.030	0.964	0.994
	12 h	-0.51399	$0.43 \cdot 10^{-4}$ $(0.84 \cdot 10^{-4})$	0.050 (0.0077)	0.927 (0.0098)	0.977	0.042	0.945	0.987
	24 h	-0.89680	$0.10 \cdot 10^{-3}$ $(0.41 \cdot 10^{-4})$	0.059 (0.0133)	0.915 (0.0199)	0.974			
GBP/USD	10 m	-0.58114	$0.10 \cdot 10^{-4}$ $(0.94 \cdot 10^{-7})$	0.160 (0.0100)	0.814 (0.0108)	0.974	0.004	0.996	1.000
	20 m	-0.95952	$0.29 \cdot 10^{-5}$ $(0.37 \cdot 10^{-6})$	0.153 (0.0124)	0.803 (0.0165)	0.956	0.006	0.994	1.000
	30 m	-1.17450	$0.55 \cdot 10^{-5}$ $(0.10 \cdot 10^{-5})$	0.153 (0.0190)	0.783 (0.0275)	0.936	0.008	0.992	1.000
	1 h	-1.54466	$0.26 \cdot 10^{-5}$ $(0.16 \cdot 10^{-5})$	0.046 (0.0174)	0.938 (0.0280)	0.984	0.010	0.988	0.998
	2 h	-1.89712	$0.67 \cdot 10^{-5}$ $(0.37 \cdot 10^{-5})$	0.050 (0.0020)	0.928 (0.0028)	0.978	0.015	0.983	0.998
	6 h	-2.45888	$0.19 \cdot 10^{-3}$ $(0.24 \cdot 10^{-4})$	0.044 (0.0040)	0.934 (0.0059)	0.978	0.026	0.967	0.993
	12 h	-0.53065	$0.49 \cdot 10^{-4}$ $(0.99 \cdot 10^{-5})$	0.043 (0.0063)	0.930 (0.0102)	0.973	0.036	0.947	0.983
	24 h	-0.91185	$0.13 \cdot 10^{-3}$ $(0.46 \cdot 10^{-4})$	0.051 (0.0072)	0.916 (0.0164)	0.967			

Table 5.1: Parameters estimates for the GARCH(1,1) with standardised maximum likelihood

Corrected standard errors are in parenthesis. The time scale is the de-seasonalised ϑ-time. The coefficients with a prime are computed from the (dis)aggregation formulas for the diffusion hypothesis. The daily interval serves as a reference basis.

rate	freq.	M.L.	α_0	α_1	β_1	$\alpha_1+\beta_1$	α_1'	β_1'	$\alpha_1'+\beta_1'$
USD/JPY	10 m	-0.54555	$0.47 \cdot 10^{-6}$ $(0.69 \cdot 10^{-7})$	0.118 (0.0074)	0.873 (0.0073)	0.991	0.006	0.994	1.000
	20 m	-0.87865	$0.11 \cdot 10^{-5}$ $(0.21 \cdot 10^{-6})$	0.123 (0.0099)	0.860 (0.0113)	0.983	0.008	0.991	0.999
	30 m	-1.08588	$0.18 \cdot 10^{-5}$ $(0.37 \cdot 10^{-6})$	0.118 (0.0138)	0.865 (0.0161)	0.983	0.010	0.989	0.999
	1 h	-1.43892	$0.31 \cdot 10^{-5}$ $(0.14 \cdot 10^{-5})$	0.091 (0.0207)	0.890 (0.0278)	0.981	0.015	0.984	0.999
	2 h	-0.01082	$0.63 \cdot 10^{-4}$ $(0.25 \cdot 10^{-4})$	0.078 (0.0024)	0.901 (0.0027)	0.979	0.020	0.976	0.996
	6 h	-2.36557	$0.16 \cdot 10^{-3}$ $(0.18 \cdot 10^{-4})$	0.057 (0.0046)	0.923 (0.0057)	0.980	0.036	0.953	0.989
	12 h	-0.40718	$0.47 \cdot 10^{-4}$ $(0.96 \cdot 10^{-4})$	0.072 (0.0100)	0.898 (0.0138)	0.970	0.050	0.927	0.977
	24 h	-0.78453	$0.14 \cdot 10^{-3}$ $(0.46 \cdot 10^{-4})$	0.072 (0.0163)	0.884 (0.0262)	0.956			
USD/CHF	10 m	-0.71958	$0.86 \cdot 10^{-6}$ $(0.97 \cdot 10^{-7})$	0.130 (0.0084)	0.854 (0.0092)	0.984	0.004	0.996	1.000
	20 m	-1.07187	$0.22 \cdot 10^{-4}$ $(0.30 \cdot 10^{-6})$	0.129 (0.0105)	0.845 (0.0128)	0.974	0.006	0.994	1.000
	30 m	-1.29173	$0.49 \cdot 10^{-5}$ $(0.87 \cdot 10^{-6})$	0.140 (0.0162)	0.817 (0.0213)	0.957	0.007	0.993	1.000
	1 h	-1.65621	$0.53 \cdot 10^{-4}$ $(0.35 \cdot 10^{-5})$	0.067 (0.0274)	0.905 (0.0446)	0.972	0.010	0.989	0.999
	2 h	-2.00321	$0.87 \cdot 10^{-4}$ $(0.52 \cdot 10^{-5})$	0.054 (0.0022)	0.923 (0.0032)	0.977	0.014	0.983	0.997
	6 h	-0.25840	$0.31 \cdot 10^{-4}$ $(0.52 \cdot 10^{-4})$	0.051 (0.0037)	0.921 (0.0046)	0.972	0.025	0.968	0.993
	12 h	-0.62878	$0.52 \cdot 10^{-4}$ $(0.28 \cdot 10^{-4})$	0.047 (0.0076)	0.930 (0.0106)	0.977	0.034	0.950	0.984
	24 h	-0.98481	$0.13 \cdot 10^{-3}$ $(0.64 \cdot 10^{-4})$	0.049 (0.0139)	0.922 (0.0243)	0.971			

Table 5.2: Parameters estimates for the GARCH(1,1) with standardised maximum likelihood

Corrected standard errors are in parenthesis. The time scale is the de-seasonalised ϑ-time. The coefficients with a prime are computed from the (dis)aggregation formulas for the diffusion hypothesis. The daily interval serves as a reference basis.

rate	freq.	M.L.	a_0	α_1	β_1	$\alpha_1+\beta_1$	α_1'	β_1'	$\alpha_1'+\beta_1'$
USD/FRF	10 m	-0.50032	$0.50 \cdot 10^{-5}$ $(0.45 \cdot 10^{-7})$	0.144 (0.0089)	0.848 (0.0083)	0.992	0.006	0.994	1.000
	20 m	-0.88450	$0.15 \cdot 10^{-4}$ $(0.25 \cdot 10^{-6})$	0.162 (0.0238)	0.826 (0.0211)	0.988	0.008	0.992	1.000
	30 m	-1.10742	$0.33 \cdot 10^{-4}$ $(0.57 \cdot 10^{-6})$	0.168 (0.0239)	0.801 (0.0242)	0.969	0.010	0.990	1.000
	1 h	-1.48620	$0.41 \cdot 10^{-4}$ $(0.5 \cdot 10^{-7})$	0.087 (0.0010)	0.888 (0.0011)	0.975	0.014	0.985	0.999
	2 h	-1.84558	$0.36 \cdot 10^{-4}$ $(0.18 \cdot 10^{-5})$	0.048 (0.0016)	0.941 (0.0016)	0.989	0.019	0.978	0.997
	6 h	-2.41546	$0.98 \cdot 10^{-4}$ $(0.11 \cdot 10^{-4})$	0.043 (0.0027)	0.946 (0.0027)	0.989	0.034	0.959	0.993
	12 h	-0.47338	$0.41 \cdot 10^{-4}$ $(0.82 \cdot 10^{-5})$	0.056 (0.0078)	0.920 (0.0104)	0.976	0.047	0.938	0.986
	24 h	-0.83423	$0.10 \cdot 10^{-3}$ $(0.35 \cdot 10^{-4})$	0.067 (0.0150)	0.904 (0.0205)	0.971			

Table 5.3: Parameters estimates for the GARCH(1,1) with standardised maximum likelihood

Corrected standard errors are in parenthesis. The time scale is the de-seasonalised ϑ-time. The coefficients with a prime are computed from the (dis)aggregation formulas for the diffusion hypothesis. The daily interval serves as a reference basis.

Chapter 6

Do Technical Trading Rules Generate Profits?

6.1 Introduction

Ever since Dow created the first market indicators in the late 1800s, technical analysis has been at the center of a debate between professionals operating in financial markets and academic economists. The latter argue that with a turnover of more than 1 trillion US dollars traded around the world every day, it is highly improbable that the foreign exchange market is not at least weakly efficient. Systematic opportunities to make profits based the analysis of past prices should be rapidly eliminated by arbitrage. More specifically, if a group of traders were to base their expectations on the extrapolation of past price trends, thereby reinforcing them, rational traders could always take a profitable speculative position based on the fundamental value, to which the exchange rate should ultimately return. In the long run, these rational traders would drive the others out of the market.

Recently, however, several researchers have overcome the natural skepticism of academics towards technical analysis in order to investigate its usefulness. Taylor and Allen (1992) surveyed more than 200 traders on the London foreign exchange market - by far the largest - and found that the use of technical analysis increases with the frequency of trading. In particular, chartism is the main forecasting tool of intradaily traders. Several other studies, including Brock et al. (1992) and Levich and Thomas (1993), have tested the potential profitability of some technical rules. Using bootstrap methods to evaluate the significance of their results, they usually found that, with daily observations, the rules they simulated would have generated some profits. In addition to providing some rationale for the actual use of technical analysis in the markets, these results could be explained on the following grounds. First, from a statistical perspective, the existence of profit-making rules might be explained by the more complex, nonlinear dynamics observed in foreign exchange rates (Hsieh, 1989; and Chapter 3). Second, it is not necessarily true that sufficient fundamental traders willing or able to take speculative positions against those using technical analysis might exist. It might well be that traders do not have sufficient liquidity or are not permitted by their institutions to take open positions for the long periods which could be needed in the event that exchange rates wander away from their fundamental values for long periods of time (International Monetary Fund, 1993). Third, the existence of other types of traders, such as central bankers, who have quite different objectives, may be at the origin of inefficiencies in the foreign exchange markets (LeBaron, 1996).

However, these studies share a number of drawbacks. First, it is yet to be shown that the profits exhibited would remain if the tests were conducted on time periods shorter than a couple of years. But, traders cannot afford to make losses during a couple of months or years even if in the extremely long run their strategies make profits. Moreover, such long periods would be in contradiction with the study of Taylor and Allen (1992) referred to above, where it was shown that technical analysis was mainly used in the very short run. Second, and using the same line of reasoning, those studies make use of daily observations whereas the bulk of foreign exchange trading - more than 75 % according to the 1996 Bank for International Settlements survey - takes place within the day; that is, between dealers and/or brokers. Third, some of these studies such as the one by Brock et al. (1992) do not incorporate transaction costs in the computation of their profits. Finally, these studies involve ex-post simulations of trading rules potentially used by traders. There is however no evidence that these rules are the ones actually used by traders. They represent only a few of a very large set of possible trading rules.

Goodhart and Curcio (1993) tried to meet this last criticism by running the following experiment. They took some students whom they divided into two groups, the first group having to trade with no external technical advice whereas the second set could rely upon the service of an existing chartist program. Although the second group did not make excess profits, they had a considerably lower variance of profits. Although it yielded interesting insights, this experiment was only a single shot. In the present chapter, we deal with the above short-comings by using buy and sell signals derived from technical rules reported by traders to Reuters. We then investigate whether intra-day trading according to these technical indicators would yield profits. For comparative purposes, we also simulate some of the rules reported in previous studies using our intradaily data set. Furthermore, the computation of profits is corrected to take account of transaction costs. Our main result is that even when transaction costs are not taken into account, it is on average not profitable to trade according to these rules, although excess returns can be made in periods of strongly trending exchange rates.

The remainder of this chapter is divided as follows. In the next section, details on the data and methodology are given. We report our results in Section 3 and give some concluding remarks in Section 4.

6.2   Data and methodology

6.2.1   Data

Our data consists of two samples, the first covering the period from 10 April 1989 to 29 June 1989 and the second running from 31 January 1994 to 30 June 1994. For each sample we have a tick-by-tick FXFX quota-

tion series for the Mark (DEM), Yen (JPY) and Pound (GBP) against
the US dollar (USD) plus daily observations on support-resistance and
HIGH-LOW trading ranges downloaded from the Reuters FXNL screen.
These trading ranges are constructed by Reuters from a daily survey of a
number of established participants in the foreign exchange markets and
represent bands within which the currency is expected to trade given information available to those participants at the beginning of the trading
day[1].

Using the tick-by-tick quotations we construct an intradaily bid, ask
and midpoint quotation series for each of the three currencies, sampled
at a fixed 1 hour calendar time interval[2]. We chose a 1-hour frequency
rather than say, a tick-by-tick or 5 minutes frequency in order to avoid
the price uncertainty due to the fact that our prices are quoted and not
transaction prices[3]. This gives a time- series length for each currency
of around 1400 return observations for the first sample and over 2500
return observations for the second sample. These intra-day quotation
series form the basis for our empirical trading rule applications.

We then combine the exchange rate data with the daily trading range
data. For the 1989 sample this is straightforward. The downloaded
trading range data is time- stamped to the second and can hence be
merged perfectly with the quotation series to give a single data set of
contemporaneous trading range and quotation series.

For the 1994 sample, however, there are two minor problems with the
trading range data. The first is that observations on all three currencies
are not available for every trading day in our sample. This leaves us
with around 90 daily observations for each currency (out of a possible
maximum number of observations of approximately 110.) Second, the
time at which the support-resistance and HIGH-LOW data was reported
by Reuters is not specified in this data set[4]. Fortunately, though, the
FXNL page which shows the trading range data also presents the prevailing spot prices for all of the selected currencies. This allows us to time
the 1994 trading range data by matching the spot prices from the FXNL
screen to those from our tick-by-tick FXFX time series, a match being

defined as a five minute interval in which all of the FXNL spot prices were simultaneously valid for the individual FXFX time-series[5]. Once this was achieved the quotation and trading range data were merged as for the 1989 sample.

Note that we assume the trading range data to be valid only until midnight on the day on which it was observed in order to avoid generating spurious buy/sell signals from stale trading range data i.e. for all hours between midnight on a given day and the observation of the next days support-resistance data the trading signal process, s_t, is restricted to be zero. This can be justified in the following ways. First,intra-day foreign exchange traders are subject to strict overnight limits on their positions; in fact they are usually expected to completely close out all positions. The restriction we place on the validity of the trading range data implicitly reflects these limits. Note however that by closing our trader's position at midnight, we implicitly allowed him to roll over his position to his overseas counterpart when both markets business hours overlap[6]. Second, a trader wishing to maintain an open position derived from a trading rule overnight will find it more costly than maintaining an intra-day position as he will have to pay overnight interest. This again implies it is more sensible to ensure that no positions can be left open overnight in our analysis.

6.2.2 The basic trading rule

Define q_t to be the quote midpoint series for the exchange rate under consideration. As mentioned above, in our empirical analyses we sample the exchange rate series at a one hour frequency. Define r_t to be the percentage return on the exchange rate, calculated as the first difference of the logarithmic mid-quotes.

All of the technical rules we employ are based on the movement of the exchange rate outside a pre-defined trading range. We present results based on four classes of trading rule definition. A first range is derived from the support and resistance levels which appear on the Reuters FXNL screen. A second possibility is to use the HIGH-LOW data which also appears on the FXNL screen. We define a third range by using both the support-resistance and HIGH-LOW data, taking the minimum of the support and LOW data and the maximum of the resistance and HIGH figures as the range. Finally, we follow Brock, Lakonishok and LeBaron (1992) in order to construct a fourth type of trading range. This range (denoted Max-Min) is calculated, at each hourly observation point, as the local maximum and minimum of the exchange rate based on a given

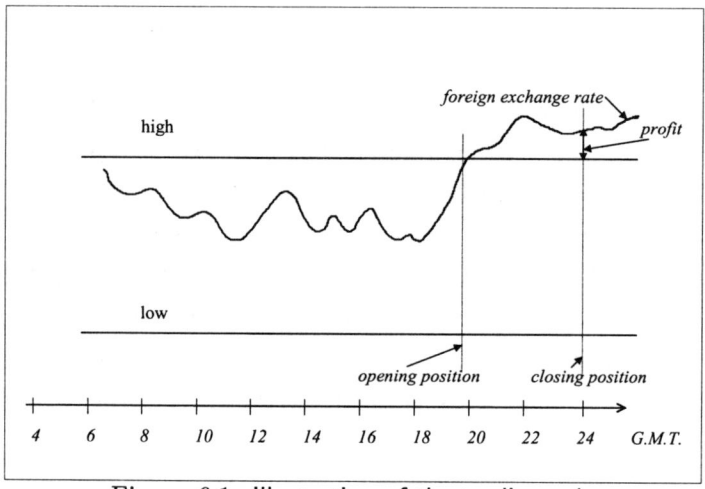

Figure 6.1: Illustration of the trading rule.

Once the trading range is defined, we can proceed to the application of the technical trading rule. Defining h_t to be the upper bound of the range and l_t to be the lower bound of the range, signals to buy and sell currency are generated according to the rule below,

$$s_t = \begin{cases} +1 & if \quad q_t > h_t \\ 0 & if \quad l_t < q_t < h_t \\ -1 & if \quad q_t < l_t \end{cases} \tag{6.1}$$

where s_t represents the signal process which is unity for a buy signal and negative one for a sell signal. Note that a purchase (sale) will be maintained until the spot rate moves back in side the upper and lower bounds (hence, the position is closed without making a profit), or until midnight on the same day, (when it is assumed that all positions are closed out for institutional reasons as in the previous discussion,) whichever is the sooner. In the first sample however, we have several updates of the lower and upper bound per day, so that profits can also be made when the exchange rates is not trending (if, for example, the upper bound is adjusted to a higher range and crossed again; in this case, the position will be closed but with a profit). Dynamic percentage returns from following this rule are simply calculated as below.

$$\pi_t = s_t(log(q_{t+1}) - log(q_t)) = s_t r_{t+1} \qquad (6.2)$$

Figure 6.1 gives an example of how such trading rule works.

In Section 3 we present data from the application of this rule to data on the DEM/USD, JPY/USD and USD/GBP. For each exchange rate, signals are generated according to the alternative range definitions and the mean return, number of buy/sell signals and a t-statistic for the significance of the mean rule return over the drift in the exchange rate return series are tabulated[8]. The t- statistic represents the significance of the trading rule return over that from a 'buy and hold' strategy and is calculated as,

$$t = \frac{\mu_T - \mu}{\left(\frac{\sigma^2}{N} + \frac{\sigma^2}{N_T}\right)^{\frac{1}{2}}} \qquad (6.3)$$

where μ_T is the mean trading rule return, μ is the mean exchange rate return, N_T is the number of trading rule signals, N is the number of exchange rate observations and $\sigma2$ is the exchange rate return variance. We also present results for a further modification of the range definitions. Indeed, traders usually modify the trading range by adding a band of variable size to the predefined range. This is the reason why this class of technical trading rules are often called filter rules. In this chapter, we add a 0.01% band to each range definition and rerun the rules. Note that like the choice of the trading range, the choice of the band is necessarily arbitrary. However, rather than the value of the band, the crucial element in a filter rule is the choice of the trading range, which is the focus of this chapter.

6.2.3   Accounting for transaction costs

The rule described above clearly takes account of neither the costs of opening and closing positions nor of the risk incurred by taking such a position. Since our trader closes his position at the latest at 12.00 p.m. G.M.T., he bears no interest costs on open positions. However, given the frequency at which one will change position in an intra-day analysis, trading costs due to bid-ask spreads are unlikely to be negligible. We (rather than using the mid-quote data as in the previous subsection) account for them by using the bid and ask quotation series. Defining a_t to be the prevailing ask quotation and b_t the bid quotation, our trading rule is redefined as,

$$s_t = \begin{cases} +1 & if & a_t > h_t \\ 0 & if & l_t < b_t, a_t < h_t \\ -1 & if & b_t < l_t \end{cases} \qquad (6.4)$$

such that a long position is established if the ask rises above the upper bound of the range and a short position taken on if the bid is below the lower bound. The real incorporation of transactions costs comes in the definition of the trading return, however. If one has, for example, taken a long position, the price at which currency was purchased was the market ask price. In closing out the position one sells back to the market, implying that one will receive the market bid. Hence, in opening and closing each position, the trader pays the quoted spread to the market maker as a transaction cost[9]. If the trading rule then determines that a position should be opened, held open for k periods and then closed, the total holding period return is then,

$$\pi_t = \begin{cases} +(log(b_{t+k}) - log(a_t)) if\, s_{t+j} = +1, \forall j = 0, ..., k-1 \\ +(log(a_{t+k}) - log(b_t)) if\, s_{t+j} = -1, \forall j = 0, ..., k-1 \end{cases} \qquad (6.5)$$

Statistics	Sample a: 10/4/89-29/6/89			Sample b: 31/1/94-30/6/94		
	DEM/USD	JPY/USD	USD/GBP	DEM/USD	JPY/USD	USD/GBP
Mean	0.0000315	0.0000573	−0.0000651	−0.0000355	−0.0000412	0.0000120
Variance	0.0000025	0.0000029	0.0000029	0.0000013	0.0000023	0.0000009
Skewness	0.134	−0.753	−0.129	−0.184	0.031	−0.043
Kurtosis	11.047	13.181	7.886	11.394	7.995	9.608
No. of Obs.	1415	1415	1415	2663	2663	2663
Trend	0.000109⋆	0.011465⋆	−0.000150⋆	−0.000047⋆	−0.001773⋆	0.000019⋆

Table 6.1: Summary statistics for hourly return series.

The row denoted trend presents the linear trend estimated in the raw mid-quote series rather than from the returns. A ⋆ indicates that the estimated trend is significantly different from zero at the 5% level.

and per-period returns are based on the above profit calculation. Results from the specifications of the trading rule which incorporate transaction costs are given in the latter half of Section 3.

6.3 Results

In Table 6.1 summary statistics are given for our two samples (hereafter referred to as 'a' and 'b'). Also, in Figures 6.2 to 6.7 we present plots of the hourly quotation series for the three currencies, for both of the sub-samples. Whilst in the second sub-sample there seems to be little evidence of global trends in the quotation series, the figures demonstrate that, for all three currencies, the first sub-sample series are subject to strong and significant trends. This observation is statistically reinforced by the estimated trends presented in the opening tables. Those for sample (a) are clearly greater than for their sample (b) counterparts.

Throughout the following section, for reasons of space, we present tables of results only for the JPY/USD exchange rate. Within the text, however, we discuss the broad results from the application of our trading rules to all three exchange rates.

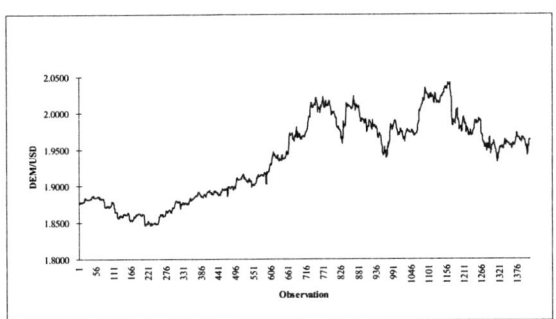

Figure 6.2: DEM/USD hourly spot exchange rate 10/4/89-29/6/89.

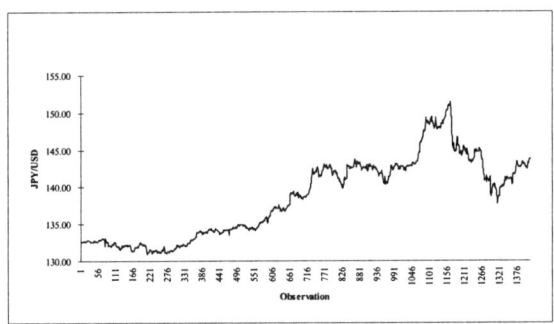

Figure 6.3: JPY/USD hourly spot exchange rate 10/4/89-29/6/89.

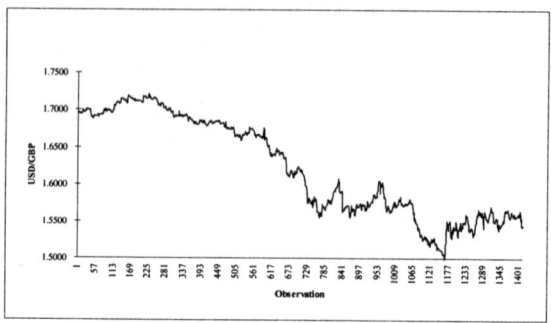

Figure 6.4: USD/GBP hourly spot exchange rate 10/4/89-29/6/89.

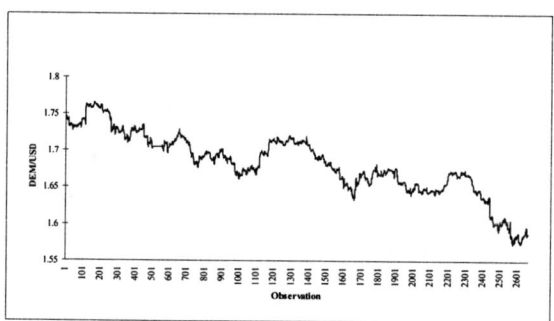

Figure 6.5: DEM/USD hourly spot exchange rate 31/1/94-30/6/94.

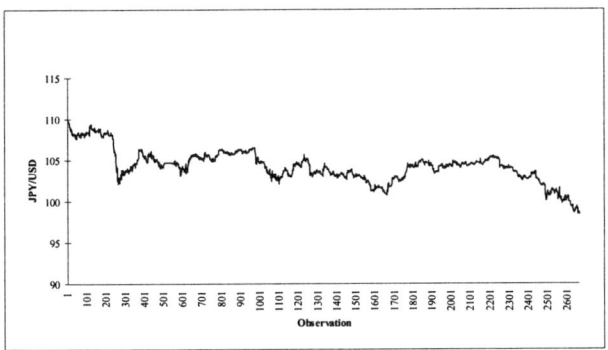

Figure 6.6: JPY/USD hourly spot exchange rate 31/1/94-30/6/94.

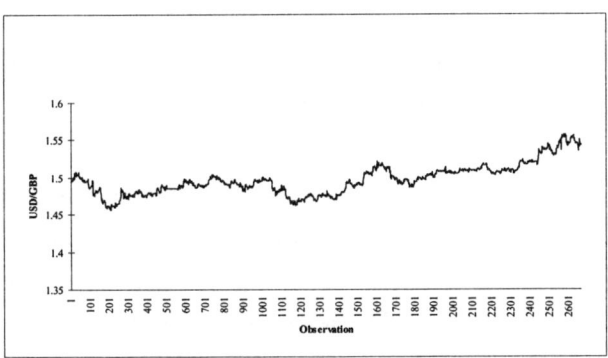

Figure 6.7: USD/GBP hourly spot exchange rate 31/1/94-30/6/94.

6.3.1   Brief summary of results from sample (a)

The first sample of intra-day exchange rates and technical rules was studied in Curcio and Goodhart (1992). Here we present a summary of their findings. Readers wanting a more complete description of the results from this sample should refer directly to Curcio and Goodhart (1992).

Results for the JPY/USD are presented in Tables 6.2 and 6.3. Examining the returns made from the application of the support-resistance and HIGH-LOW rules to these data (Table 6.2) demonstrates that in the majority of cases they are positive and are generally an order of magnitude greater than the returns from a buy and hold strategy. Examining the significance of the buy and sell sides separately, one finds that in 18 of the 36 cases the rules generate significant profit. Further, amalgamating the buy and sell sides for each rule, of the 18 returns across the three currencies, 12 are significantly greater than zero.

Similar results obtain for the application of the Max-Min rules proposed by Brock, Lakonishok and LeBaron (1992) (presented for the JPY/USD in Table 6.3), although they are slightly weaker. Profits are positive for only 14 of the 36 separate buy and sell rules, and the composite buy-sell return is significantly greater than zero in 8 of the 18 cases.

Hence, it seems that there are rules which, when applied to our first intra-day exchange rate sample, could have made consistently positive profits. A more careful examination of the results, however, demonstrates that the significance of these rules is entirely asymmetric. Examining the support-resistance results, for the DEM/USD and JPY/USD all buy side rules are significant and none of the sell rules are, whilst the opposite holds for the USD/GBP. A similar conclusion holds when one examines the Max-Min results, with the sells being the only significantly profitable rules for the USD/GBP and the buys for the DEM/USD and JPY/USD.

These results can be linked to the trend in our exchange rate sample. As mentioned earlier, sample (a) covers a period of sustained USD

Series	Side of Market	No transaction costs			With transaction costs		
		Number	Mean	t-stat	Number	Mean	t-stat
Returns	—	1415	0.005727	—	1415	$5.68 \cdot 10^{-5}$	—
$S - R$	Buy	179	0.032337	1.96⋆	225	$5.05 \cdot 10^{-5}$	−0.05203
	Sell	111	0.005298	−0.03	108	$7.39 \cdot 10^{-5}$	0.787187
	Composite	290	0.021988	1.47	333	$5.81 \cdot 10^{-5}$	0.013474
$H - L$	Buy	188	0.038528	2.47⋆	215	0.000228	1.410818
	Sell	121	0.010541	0.30	122	$6.17 \cdot 10^{-5}$	0.75485
	Composite	309	0.027569	2.85⋆	337	0.000168	1.104558
Both	Buy	120	0.052711	2.88⋆	143	0.000291	1.606613
	Sell	75	0.015384	0.48	73	0.000183	1.204033
	Composite	195	0.038354	2.03⋆	216	0.000255	1.630343
$S - R + 0.1\%$	Buy	121	0.066373	3.74⋆	147	0.000255	1.375831
	Sell	86	0.007993	0.12	76	0.000105	0.828635
	Composite	207	0.042119	1.74	223	0.000204	1.229398
$H - L + 0.1\%$	Buy	127	0.051268	2.87⋆	149	0.000314	1.799477
	Sell	100	−0.00371	−0.53	93	0.000129	1.0417
	Composite	227	0.027049	2.49⋆	242	0.000243	1.610659
$Both + 0.1\%$	Buy	88	0.063721	3.08⋆	100	0.00047	2.401244⋆
	Sell	61	0.022457	0.75	53	0.000312	1.585821
	Composite	149	0.046828	2.79⋆	153	0.000415	2.533395⋆

Table 6.2: JPY/USD trading rule results, sample a.

appreciation, implying a strong upward trend in the DEM/USD and JPY/USD whilst the USD/GBP trended downward over our sample. As the filter rules which we employ are essentially trend-following rules, the significance and asymmetry of our results may be attributed to the strong trends in our exchange rate sample. This behaviour can also be seen in the number of signals generated. For the JPY/USD, for example, Table 1 demonstrates that there are far more buys than sells JPY/USD, a result which also holds for the DEM/USD whilst the converse is true for the USD/GBP. This, again, can be seen as indicative of the trend-chasing nature of our trading rules.

A further qualification to our result that application of these rules

Series	Side of Market	No transaction costs			With transaction costs		
		Number	Mean	t-stat	Number	Mean	t-stat
Returns	–	1415	0.005727	–	1415	$5.68 \cdot 10^{-5}$	–
50	Buy	145	0.032823	1.81	140	0.000163	0.72
	Sell	63	−0.01832	−1.09	53	−0.00031	−1.08
	Composite	208	0.017333	0.91	193	$3.33 \cdot 10^{-5}$	−0.18
150	Buy	111	0.038047	1.91	101	0.000263	1.20
	Sell	21	0.004158	−0.04	12	−0.00012	−0.14
	Composite	132	0.032656	1.33	113	0.000222	1.02
200	Buy	102	0.0398	1.94	95	0.000264	1.18
	Sell	13	0.005589	0.00	4	−0.00036	−0.37
	Composite	115	0.035933	1.73	99	0.000239	1.05
50 + 0.1%	Buy	60	0.064038	2.58⋆	47	0.000378	1.31
	Sell	36	−0.02741	−1.15	24	−0.00064	−1.69
	Composite	96	0.029745	1.73	71	$3.55 \cdot 10^{-5}$	−0.11
150 + 0.1%	Buy	48	0.063098	2.28⋆	37	0.000458	1.45
	Sell	16	−0.01487	−0.48	8	−0.00062	−0.96
	Composite	64	0.043606	1.83	45	0.000265	0.83
200 + 0.1%	Buy	48	0.063098	2.28*	37	0.000458	1.45
	Sell	16	−0.022	−0.56	4	−0.00036	−0.37
	Composite	64	0.041824	1.79	41	0.000378	1.22

Table 6.3: JPY/USD max-min results, sample a.

generates excess returns is that the analysis thus far does not account for transaction costs. As described in Section 2, we embody these costs by incorporating the bid-ask spread into our return calculations. The results for the JPY/USD which correspond to our rules which include transaction costs are given in the final three columns of Tables 6.2 and 6.3. A general result which emerges from examination of these tables is that, once spreads are accounted for, virtually all trading rule profits are eliminated. For the Reuters trading range data, only 4 of the 36 buy or sell rules yield returns which are significantly greater than zero at conventional levels. Further, only 2 of the 18 composite bid and ask rules have significantly positive returns. As before, the returns from the

Max-Min rules are poorer than the returns from the Reuters based rules; none are significantly greater than zero, whilst 7 of the 36 separate bid and ask rules and two of the composite rules yield significant losses.

6.3.2 Results from sample (b)

Examining results for our second sample of exchange rates and technical rules gives a far more dismal picture of the profitability of these techniques. In comparison to those from sample (a), the results are sketchy and inconsistent. A source of this difference is likely to be the difference between the strength of the exchange rate trends across the two samples.

Specific observations on the application of the support-resistance and HIGH-LOW rules are as follows (see Table 6.4 for JPY/USD results). In only the USD/GBP case is there any indication of more signals being generated for one side of the market than for the other (in this case buy signals seem to predominate.) Only 15 of the 36 separate buy and sell returns are positive and of these only 4 are significant. In fact, there are almost as many significantly negative returns (3 of 36) as there are significantly positive returns. Further, only 2 of the 18 composite buy and sell rules yield significant profits. Again the results from the application of the Max-Min rules are weaker (see Table 6.5). Only 9 rules generate positive returns and there are far more significantly negative returns (7) than significantly positive (2). This leads to the result that only one composite return yields excess returns significantly greater than zero, whilst 4 of the 18 yield significant losses.

For sample (b) all the significant profits accrue from the application of technical rules to the JPY/USD exchange rate. As can be seen from Figure 6.6, the JPY was subject to two sharp periods of appreciation, at the beginning and end of the sample. In line with the results from sample (a) we hypothesise that these episodes might be the source of the positive profits and test this hypothesis below.

Our test consists simply of dividing sample (b) into periods in which strong trends pertain in the exchange rates and periods of no trend. This type of exercise is far less easy for sample (a) where it seems that

Series	Side of Market	No transaction costs			With transaction costs		
		Number	Mean	t-stat	Number	Mean	t-stat
Returns	–	2663	$-4.12 \cdot 10^{-5}$	–	2663	$-4.12 \cdot 10^{-5}$	–
S − R	Buy	103	-0.00014	-0.64	106	-0.00026	-1.37
	Sell	89	0.000362	$1.96\star$	97	$9.92 \cdot 10^{-5}$	0.35
	Composite	192	$9.35 \cdot 10^{-5}$	1.22	203	$-8.7 \cdot 10^{-5}$	0.39
H − L	Buy	226	$-9.58 \cdot 10^{-5}$	-0.52	242	-0.00025	-1.92
	Sell	226	0.000259	$2.07\star$	234	0.000138	0.89
	Composite	452	$8.16 \cdot 10^{-5}$	1.60	476	$-5.7 \cdot 10^{-5}$	-0.20
Both	Buy	88	-0.0002	-0.98	93	-0.00037	$-1.97\star$
	Sell	84	0.000422	2.26	92	0.000147	0.63
	Composite	172	0.000102	1.23	185	-0.00011	-0.60
S − R + 0.1%	Buy	69	-0.00022	-0.94	82	-0.00019	-0.85
	Sell	53	0.000216	0.83	68	0.000282	1.24
	Composite	122	$-2.8 \cdot 10^{-5}$	0.11	150	$2.29 \cdot 10^{-5}$	0.48
H − L + 0.1%	Buy	149	-0.00011	-0.56	168	-0.00038	$-2.72\star$
	Sell	184	0.000341	$2.59\star$	197	0.000146	0.90
	Composite	333	0.000138	$2.04\star$	365	$-9.8 \cdot 10^{-5}$	-0.64
Both + 0.1%	Buy	56	-0.00023	-0.90	67	-0.00036	-1.65
	Sell	52	0.000235	0.91	63	0.000366	1.61
	Composite	108	$-4 \cdot 10^{-6}$	0.26	130	$-1 \cdot 10^{-5}$	0.22

Table 6.4: JPY trading rule results, sample b.

all three exchange rates are trended over the entire period. This is also true, to a lesser extent, for the DEM/USD in sample (b). The division leaves us with a 'flat' and 'trended' sub-sample for each of the JPY/USD and USD/GBP in sample (b)[10]. Unfortunately, the 'trend' sub-sample for the USD/GBP contained too few signals for reliable statistical inference and we hence present tables which only cover the JPY/USD sub-samples.

Results from the application of the support-resistance rules to these sub-samples are shown in Tables 6.6 and 6.7 and they immediately bear out our intuition regarding the source of trading rule profits. The 'flat' JPY/USD sub-sample shows all buy and sell returns to be negative

Series	Side of Market	No transaction costs			With transaction costs		
		Number	Mean	t-stat	Number	Mean	t-stat
Returns	–	2663	$-4.12 \cdot 10^{-5}$	–	2663	$-4.12 \cdot 10^{-5}$	–
50	Buy	139	-0.00021	-1.29	128	-0.00084	$-5.56\star$
	Sell	174	$5.15 \cdot 10^{-6}$	0.30	167	-0.00028	$-2.52\star$
	Composite	313	$-9.1 \cdot 10^{-5}$	-0.56	295	-0.00052	$-4.94\star$
150	Buy	66	-0.00022	-0.95	55	-0.00082	$-3.59\star$
	Sell	110	0.000721	$4.60\star$	105	-0.00016	-1.29
	Composite	176	0.000367	$3.49\star$	160	-0.00039	$-2.68\star$
200	Buy	48	-0.00019	-0.65	40	-0.00077	$-2.87\star$
	Sell	109	$5.82 \cdot 10^{-5}$	0.11	104	-0.00015	-1.19
	Composite	157	$-1.6 \cdot 10^{-5}$	0.19	144	-0.00032	$-2.05\star$
50 + 0.1%	Buy	47	-0.00058	$-2.42\star$	46	-0.00161	$-6.65\star$
	Sell	78	$8.61 \cdot 10^{-5}$	0.26	78	-0.00045	$-2.72\star$
	Composite	125	-0.00016	-0.95	124	-0.00088	$-5.78\star$
150 + 0.1%	Buy	18	-0.00043	-1.08	16	-0.00121	$-2.95\star$
	Sell	54	0.000121	0.38	55	-0.00036	-1.86
	Composite	72	$-1.6 \cdot 10^{-5}$	0.07	71	-0.00055	$-2.68\star$
200 + 0.1%	Buy	15	-0.0003	-0.66	13	-0.00107	$-2.34\star$
	Sell	52	0.00016	0.56	53	-0.00031	-1.57
	Composite	67	$5.65 \cdot 10^{-5}$	0.47	66	-0.00046	$-2.10\star$

Table 6.5: JPY max-min results, sample b.

with, obviously, no significant trading rule profits. For the 'trend' sub-sample though, the appreciation of the JPY can be seen to generate significant profits for the sell-side rules. Hence it seems that these rules only generate consistent profits when there are strong trends in exchange rates. If one therefore desired to apply them practically, one would not only have to know the correct rule to implement, but also when to apply the rule in terms of the start points of possible exchange rate trends.

Finally, incorporating transaction costs into the analysis inevitably makes the results even more convincing of market efficiency. Simply incorporating the spread (as a transaction cost) into our calculations eliminates all significantly positive returns for the full sample (b) series.

Series		Number	Mean	t-stat
Returns	—	1929	$1.34 \cdot 10^{-5}$	—
$S - R$	Buy	97	−0.00014	−1.03
	Sell	42	−0.00014	−0.57
	Composite	139	−0.00014	−1.22
$H - L$	Buy	208	$-8.18 \cdot 10^{-5}$	−0.90
	Sell	142	$-4.11 \cdot 10^{-6}$	-0.07
	Composite	350	$-5 \cdot 10^{-5}$	−0.76
Both	Buy	85	−0.00018	−1.23
	Sell	37	$-7.45 \cdot 10^{-5}$	−0.25
	Composite	122	−0.00015	−1.22
$S - R + 0.1\%$	Buy	63	−0.00023	−1.30
	Sell	18	−0.0006	−1.71
	Composite	81	−0.00031	−1.97⋆
$H - L + 0.1\%$	Buy	138	$-9.62 \cdot 10^{-5}$	−0.86
	Sell	105	$-5.47 \cdot 10^{-5}$	−0.29
	Composite	243	$-7.8 \cdot 10^{-5}$	−0.93
Both + 0.1%	Buy	56	−0.00023	−1.22
	Sell	17	−0.00059	−1.63
	Composite	73	−0.00031	−1.88

Table 6.6: Flat JPY sub-sample trading rule results, sample b.

For the support-resistance rules only 10 applications have positive returns at all, whilst 14 returns are significantly negative. The Max-Min results all show negative returns, with 32 of the 36 being significantly negative.

Hence, the main points from all our results are as follows. Sample (a) indicates that significant profits can be made from the application of these trading rules, whilst sample (b) indicates the opposite. This difference in results can be explained in terms of the strength of the

Series		Number	Mean	t-stat
Returns	–	734	-0.00018	–
$S - R$	Buy	6	$-9.16 \cdot 10^{-5}$	0.13
	Sell	47	0.000812	2.47$\star$
	Composite	53	0.00071	3.72$\star$
$H - L$	Buy	18	-0.00026	-0.18
	Sell	83	0.000712	2.70$\star$
	Composite	101	0.00054	4.04$\star$
Both	Buy	3	-0.00075	-0.58
	Sell	47	0.000812	2.47$\star$
	Composite	50	0.000718	3.66$\star$
$S - R + 0.1\%$	Buy	6	$-9.16 \cdot 10^{-5}$	0.13
	Sell	35	0.000634	1.54
	Composite	41	0.000528	2.63$\star$
$H - L + 0.1\%$	Buy	11	-0.00033	-0.28
	Sell	78	0.000877	3.44$\star$
	Composite	89	0.000728	4.82$\star$
$Both + 0.1\%$	Buy	–	–	–
	Sell	35	0.000634	1.54
	Composite	35	0.000634	1.54

Table 6.7: Trended JPY sub-sample trading rule results, sample b.

trend in exchange rates in the two samples. Trading rule application can be profitable in trending markets. This, however, does not make the task of generating profits any easier; in order to derive profitable returns from technical analysis one not only has to pick an appropriate rule, but must also be able to identify the start points of sustained trends in foreign exchange rates. Further results suggest that, on average, the support-resistance rules perform better than the Max-Min rules used in Brock, Lakonishok and LeBaron (1992) and that, regardless of the strength of the trend in the exchange rate, once transaction costs are accounted for no rule generates significant profits.

6.4   Conclusion

In this chapter, we have evaluated the profitability of trading strategies based on the application of support and resistance provided by traders to Reuters in the intradaily foreign exchange market. We also simulated some of the technical rules used in former studies. Our main result is that, on average, neither of these sets of rules generate profitable trading strategies. Our result is even more significant when we take transaction costs into account. However, this result requires a number of qualifications. First, as - quite naturally - some profitability could be achieved for the sub-periods where a trend could be observed in the data, one may argue that traders would actually act upon the trading signals reported on Reuters only in periods where such trends are present. Indeed, although the buy and sell signals are the ones reported by traders, we have no figures on the volume traded on these signals. Second, even though these signals are ones reported by traders, it is unlikely that they are the only ones that they use. As well as the filter rules applied in this chapter there are at least two other main classes of chartist rules, namely rules based on the crossing of moving averages and rules based on so-called momentums. Third, Surajaras and Sweeney (1992) for example have argued that the use of portfolio strategies based on trading several currencies are likely to be more profitable. However, most intra-day foreign exchange traders, whether dealers or brokers, specialise in a single exchange rate. Bearing these words of caution in mind, our results are nevertheless consistent with efficiency in the foreign exchange market.

Footnotes

(1) Note that, although it could be argued that traders have no incentive to report their best estimates, they also know that their estimates will be diluted in the aggregation of responses implying incentives to misreport are likely to be diminished or removed.

(2) Our analysis excludes weekends, defined as midnight on Friday to midnight Sunday GMT.

(3) See Chapter 2 for a discussion of this issue.

(4) Note that the trading range observations for all three currencies are simultaneously reported by Reuters.

(5) In some cases there were multiple matches for a given daily observation. We countered this problem by running all our trading rules using daily trading range data defined from the first match-time in each day, the average and finally the last. Our results were almost identical across these three definitions and we present results based on the first possible match in the rest of this chapter.

(6) Positions could be rolled over by a Japanese trader to his European counterpart or by an European trader to his American counterpart. We closed the position at 12.00 when there is no overlap between the American and Japanese markets.

(7) Again following Brock, Lakonishok and LeBaron (1992) the horizons we employ are 50, 150 and 200 observations.

(8) It is well known that the distribution of exchange rate returns deviates fairly significantly from the normal. This implies that a more appropriate way of testing the significance of trading rule returns would be to use a bootstrap, as in Brock, Lakonishok and LeBaron (1992). However the results in Brock, Lakonishok and LeBaron (1992) are not qualitatively altered by using bootstrapped standard errors and hence we focus on traditional t-statistics to provide statistical inference.

(9) Note that the bid and ask data we employ are taken from Reuters FXFX screens. It has become a well recognized fact that the spreads quoted on these screens bracket the true inside spreads in the inter-

dealer market, implying that our measure of transactions costs might be slightly overstated.

(10) The trended JPY/USD sub-samples cover observations 1-250 and 2200-2663 approximately. The trended USD/GBP sub-sample covers observations 1750-2663.

Bibliography

Admati A. R. and Pfleiderer P., 1988, *A theory of intraday patterns: volume and price variability*, The Review of Financial Studies, **1**, 3–40.

Albano A., Muench J., and Schwartz C., 1988, *Singular-value decomposition and the grassberger-procaccia algorithm*, Physical Review A, **38**, 3017–3026.

Allais M., 1974, *The psychological rate of interest*, Journal of Money, Credit and Banking, **3**, 285–331.

Andersen T. G., 1992, *Return volatility and trading volume: an information flow interpretation of stochastic volatility*, Kellogg Graduate School of Management, Northwestern University, **working paper 170**, 1–35.

Andersen T. G. and Bollerslev T., 1997, *Heterogeneous information arrivals and return volatility dynamics: uncovering the long-run in high frequency returns*, Journal of Finance, **52**, 975–1006.

Ashley R., Patterson D., and Hinich M., 1986, *A diagnostic test for nonlinear serial dependence in time series fitting errors*, Journal of Time Series Analysis, **7**, 165–178.

Baillie R. T. and Bollerslev T., 1989, *The message in daily exchange rates: a conditional-variance tale*, Journal of Business and Economic Statistics, **7**(3), 297–305.

Baillie R. T. and Bollerslev T., 1990, *Intra day and inter market volatility in foreign exchange rates*, Review of Economic Studies, **58**, 565–585.

Baillie R. T., Bollerslev T., and Mikkelsen H.-O., 1993, *Fractionally integrated generalized autoregressive conditional heteroskedasticity*, Kellogg Graduate School of Management, Northwestern University, **working paper 168**, 1–24.

Baillie R. T. and McMahon P. C., 1989, *The foreign exchange market*, Cambridge University Press, Cambridge.

Bajo-Rubio O., Fernandez-Rodriguez F., and Sosvilla-Rivera S., 1992, *Chaotic behaviour in exchange series*, Economics Letters, **39**, 207–211.

Bank for International Settlements, 1993, *Central bank survey of foreign exchange market activity*, document from the Monetary and Economic Department, **Basle February 1993**, 1–42.

Barnett W. and Chen P., 1988, *The aggregation-theoretic monetary aggregates are chaotic and have strange attractors*, in W. Barnett, E. Berndt and H. White (eds), Dynamic econometric modelling, Cambridge University Press, 199–245.

Berndt E., Hall B., Hall R., and Hausman J., 1974, *Estimation and inference in nonlinear structural models*, Annals of Economic and Social Measurement, **3**, 653–665.

Bewley T., 1986, *Dynamic implications of the form of the budget constraint*, in H. Sonnenschein (ed.), Models of Economic Dynamics, Springer-Verlag, 105–134.

Blank S., 1991, *Chaos in futures markets? a nonlinear dynamical analysis*, Journal of Futures Markets, **11**, 711–728.

Boldrin M. and Woodford M., 1990, *Equilibrium models displaying endogenous fluctuations and chaos, a survey*, Journal of Monetary Economics, **25**, 189–222.

Bollerslev T., 1986, *Generalized autoregressive conditional heteroskedasticity*, Journal of Econometrics, **31**, 307–327.

Bollerslev T., Chou R. Y., and Kroner K. F., 1992, *ARCH modeling in finance*, Journal of Econometrics, **52**, 5–59.

Bollerslev T. and Domowitz I., 1993, *Trading patterns and prices in the interbank foreign exchange market*, The Journal of Finance, **48**, 1421–1443.

Bollerslev T. and Melvin M., 1994, *Bid-ask spreads and volatility in the foreign exchange market: an empirical analysis*, Journal of International Economics, **36**, 355–372.

Boothe P. and Glassman D., 1987, *The statistical distribution of exchange rates, empirical evidence and economic implications*, Journal of International Economics, **22**, 297–319.

Branson W. and Henderson D., 1985, *The specification and influence in asset markets*, in R. Jones and P. Kenen (eds.), "Handbook of International Economics, **2**, 749–805.

Brock W., Lakonishok J., and LeBaron B., 1992a, *Simple technical trading rules and the stochastic properties of stock returns*, The Journal of Finance, **47**(5), 1731–1764.

Brock W. A. and Dechert D., 1991, *Nonlinear dynamical systems: instability and chaos in economics*, in W. Hildenbrand and H. Sonnenschein (eds), Handbook of Mathemathical Economics IV, North-Holland, 2209–2235.

Brock W. A., Dechert W., and Scheinkman J., 1987, *A test for independence based on the correlation dimension*, SSRI Working Paper, Department of Economics, University of Wisconsin, Madison, **8762**, 1–16.

Brock W. A., Hsieh D. A., and LeBaron B., 1992b, *Nonlinear dynamics, chaos, and instability: statistical theory and economic evidence*, MIT Press, Cambridge, Massachussets.

Broomhead D. and King G., 1986a, *Extracting qualitative dynamics from experimental data*, Physica D, **20**, 217–236.

Broomhead D. and King G., 1986b, *On the qualitative analysis of experimental dynamical systems*, in S. Sarkar (ed), Nonlinear phenomena and chaos, Hilger Bristol, 113–144.

Calderon-Rossel J. R. and Ben-Horim M., 1982, *The behavior of the foreign exchange rates, empirical evidence and economic implications*, Journal of International Business Studies, **13**, 99–111.

Chan K. and Tong H., 1994, *A note on noisy chaos*, to appear in Journal of Royal Statistical Society, **56**.

Chauveau T. and Topol R., 1993, *Exchange rate dynamics with heterogeneous beliefs: a theoretical justification of some assymmetric arch effects*, Unpublished manuscript. Organisme Francais de Conjoncture Economique, 1–45.

Chen S., 1992, *A model of endogenous fluctuations of real exchange rates*, Unpublished Ph.D. thesis. Department of Economics. Yale University, 1–35.

Chiarella C., 1990, *Excessive exchange rate variability, a possible explanation using nonlinear economic dynamics*, European Journal of Political Economy, **6**, 315–352.

Clark P. K., 1973, *A subordinated stochastic process model with finite variance for speculative prices*, Econometrica, **41**(1), 135–155.

Cox J. C. and Rubinstein M., 1985, *Options Markets*, Prentice-Hall, New Jersey.

Curcio R. and Goodhart C., 1992, *When support/resistance levels are broken, can profits be made? evidence from the foreign exchange market*, London School of Economics - Financial Markets Group Discussion Paper, **142**, 1–22.

Dacorogna M. M., Gauvreau C. L., Müller U. A., Olsen R. B., and Pictet O. V., 1996, *Changing time scale for short-term forecasting in financial markets*, Journal of Forecasting, **15**, 203–227.

Dacorogna M. M., Müller U. A., Nagler R. J., Olsen R. B., and Pictet O. V., 1993, *A geographical model for the daily and weekly seasonal volatility in the FX market*, Journal of International Money and Finance, **12**(4), 413–438.

Dacorogna M. M., Pictet O. V., Müller U. A., and de Vries C. G., 1994, *The distribution of extremal foreign exchange rate returns in extremely large data sets*, Internal document UAM.1992-10-22, Olsen & Associates, Seefeldstrasse 233, 8008 Zürich, Switzerland.

Dacorogna M. M., Pictet O. V. H., Müller U. A., and De Vries C. G., 1997, *The distribution of extremal exchange rate returns and extremely large data sets*, unpublished manuscript, Olsen & Associates.

Danielsson J. and Payne R., 1999, *Real trading patterns and prices in spot foreign exchange markets*, unpublished manuscript, Financial Markets Group, London School of Economics.

Davé R. D., 1993, *Statistical correlation of data frequency price change and spread results*, Internal document RDD.1993-04-26, Olsen & Associates, Seefeldstrasse 233, 8008 Zürich, Switzerland.

de Haan L., 1990, *Fighting the arch-enemy with mathematics*, Statistica Neerlandica, **44**, 45–68.

de Vries C. G., 1994, *Stylized facts of nominal exchange rate returns*, in Handbook of International Macroeconomics, F. van der Ploeg (ed.), 348–389.

Dechert W. and Gencay R., 1992, *Lyapunov exponents as a nonparametric diagnostic for stability analysis*, Journal of Applied Econometrics, **7**, S41–S60.

DeCoster G. and Mitchell D., 1991, *Nonlinear monetary dynamics*, Journal of Business and Economic Statistics, **9**, 455–461.

DeGrauwe P. and Dewachter H., 1993, *A chaotic model of the exchange rate: the role of fundamentalists and chartists*, Open economies review, **4**, 351–379.

DeGrauwe P., Janssens M., and Leliaert H., 1985, *Real exchange rate variability from 1920 to 1926 and 1973 to 1982*, Princeton Studies in International Finance, **56**.

Demos A. A. and Goodhart C. A. E., 1992, *The interaction between the frequency of market quotations,spread, and volatility in the foreign exchange market*, LSE Financial Markets Group Discussion Paper, **152**, 1–38.

Destexhe A., Sepulchre J., and Babloyantz A., 1988, *A comparative study of the experimental quantification of deterministic chaos*, Physical Letters A, **132**, 101–106.

Dewachter H. and Guillaume D., 1992, *Is there deterministic chaos in the foreign exchange markets?*, mimeo , Catholic University of Leuven.

Diebold F. X. and Nason J. A., 1990, *Nonparametric exchange rate prediction?*, Journal of International Economics, **28**, 315–332.

Ding Z., Granger C. W. J., and Engle R. F., 1993, *A long memory property of stock market returns and a new model*, Journal of Empirical Finance, **1**, 83–106.

Drost F. and Nijman T., 1993, *Temporal aggregation of garch processes*, Econometrica, **61**, 909–927.

Eben K., 1994, *Arbitrage alerts and changing interrelations between fx-rates*, unpublished manuscript, Institute of Computer Science, Academy of Sciences of the Czech Republic.

Eckmann J. and Ruelle D., 1992, *Fundamental limitations for estimating dimensions and Lyapunov exponents in dynamical systems*, Physica D, **56**, 185–187.

Eckmann J.-P., Kamphorst S., Ruelle D., and Scheinkman J., 1988, *Lyapunov exponents for stock returns*, in P. Anderson, K. Arrow and D. Pines (eds), The economy as an evolving complex system, Santa Fe Institute studies in the sciences of complexities, Addison-Wesley, 301–304.

Eckmann J.-P. and Ruelle D., 1985, *Ergodic theory of chaos and strange attractors*, Review of Modern Physics, **57**, 617–656.

Edison H., 1993, *The effectiveness of central bank intervention: a survey of the Post-1982 literature*, Essays in International Finance. Princeton University.

Engle C. and Hamilton J., 1990, *Long swings in the foreign exchange market: are they there, and do investors know it?*, American Economic Review, **80**, 689–713.

Engle R. F., 1982, *Autoregressive conditional heteroskedasticity with estimates of the variance of U. K. inflation*, Econometrica, **50**, 987–1008.

Engle R. F., Ito T., and Lin W.-L., 1990, *Meteor showers or heat waves? Heteroskedastic intra-daily volatility in the foreign exchange market*, Econometrica, **58**, 525–542.

Engle R. F., Ito T., and Lin W.-L., 1992, *Where does the meteor shower come from ? the role of stochastic policy coordination*, Journal of International Economics, **32**, 221–240.

Fama E., 1965, *The behavior of stock market prices*, Journal of Business, 34–105.

Feller W., 1971, *An Introduction to Probability Theory and Its Applications*, volume II of *Wiley Series in Probability and Mathematical Statistics*, John Wiley, New York, 2nd edition.

Flood M. D., 1994, *Market structure and inefficiency in the foreign exchange market,* Journal of International Money and Finance, **13**(2), 131–158.

Flood R. and Hodrick R., 1990, *On testing for speculative bubbles,* Journal of Economic Perspectives, **4**, 85–101.

Fraedrich K. and Wang R., 1993, *Estimating the correlation dimension of an attractor from noisy and small datasets based on re-embedding,* Physica D, **65**, 373–398.

Frank M. and Stengos T., 1989, *Measuring the strangeness of gold and silver rates of return,* Review of Economic Studies, **56**, 553–567.

Frankel J. and Rose A., 1995, *Empirical research on nominal exchange rates,* in Grossman G. and K. Rogoff (Eds.) Handbook of International Economics., **3**(1689-1729), 317–326.

Fraser A. and Swinney H., 1986, *Independent coordinates for strange attractors from mutual information,* Physical Review A, **33**, 1134–1140.

Frenkel J. and Mussa M., 1985, *Asset markets, exchange rates and the balance of payments,* in R. Jones and P. Kenen (eds.), "Handbook of International Economics, **2**, 679–747.

Froot K. and Thaler R., 1990, *Anomalies. foreign exchange,* Journal of Economic Perspectives, **4**, 179–202.

Gallant A., 1981, *On the bias in flexible functional forms and an essentially unbiased form: the fourier flexible form,* Journal of Econometrics, **15**, 211–245.

Gallez D. and Babloyantz A., 1991, *Lyapunov exponents for nonuniform attractors,* Physics Letters, **161**, 247–254.

Garman M., 1976, *Market microstructure,* Journal of Financial Economics, **3**, 257–275.

Ghysels E. and Jasiak J., 1994, *Stochastic volatility and time deformation: an application of trading volume and leverage effects*, C.R.D.E. and Departement des Sciences Economiques, Universite de Montreal.

Gielens G., Straetmans S., and de Vries C. G., 1995, *Fat tail distributions and local thin tail alternatives*, Mimeo, Tinbergen Instituut Rotterdam, 1–14.

Goldberg D. E., 1989, *Genetic Algorithms in Search, Optimization & Machine Learning*, Addison-Wesley, Reading, Massachusetts.

Goldberg M. and Frydman R., 1993, *Qualitative rationality and behavior in the foreign exchange market*, Unpublished manuscript. Department of Economics. New York University, 1–35.

Goodhart C., Ito T., and Payne R., 1995, *One day in june, 1993: a study of the working of the reuters dealing 2000-2 electronic foreign exchange trading system*, mimeo, London School of Economics, 1–36.

Goodhart C. A., 1989, *'news' and the foreign exchange market*, Proceedings of the Manchester Statistical Society, 1–79.

Goodhart C. A. and Demos A., 1990, *Reuters screen images of the foreign exchange market: the deutschemark/dollar spot rate*, Journal of International Securities Markets, **4**, 333–348.

Goodhart C. A. and Figliuoli L., 1992, *The geographical location of the foreign exchange market: a test of an "islands" hypothesis*, Journal of International and Comparative Economics, **1**, 13–27.

Goodhart C. A. E. and Figliuoli L., 1991, *Every minute counts in financial markets*, Journal of International Money and Finance, **10**, 23–52.

Goodhart C. A. E., Hall S. G., Henry S. G. B., and Pesaran B., 1993, *News effects in a high frequency model of the sterling-dollar exchange rate*, Journal of Applied Econometrics, **8**, 1–13.

Goodhart C. A. E. and Hesse T., 1993, *Central Bank Forex intervention assessed in continuous time*, Journal of International Money and Finance, **12**(4), 368–389.

Goodhart C. C. and Curcio R., 1991, *The clustering of bid/ask prices and the spread in the foreign exchange market*, LSE Financial Market Group Discussion Paper Series, **110**, 1–15.

Grandmont J., 1985, *On endogenous competitive business cycles*, Econometrica, **53**, 995–1045.

Grandmont J. and Laroque G., 1986, *Stability of cycles and expectations*, Journal of Economic Theory, **40**, 138–151.

Grandmont J.-M., 1992, *Expectations driven nonlinear business cycles*, to appear in Proceedings of the Stockholm Conference (FIEF papers).

Granger C. and Ding Z., 1993, *Some properties of absolute return: An alternative measure of risk*, presented at the conference on 'Financial markets dynamics and forecasting', organized by the Groupe Caisse des depots and G.R.E.Q.E., 1–30.

Grassberger P., 1990, *An optimized box-assisted algorithm for fractal dimensions*, Physics Letters A, **148**, 63–68.

Grassberger P. and Procaccia I., 1983a, *Characterization of strange attractors*, Physical Review Letters, **50**, 346–349.

Grassberger P. and Procaccia I., 1983b, *Measuring the strangeness of strange attractors*, Physica D, **9**, 189–208.

Grassberger P., Schreiber T., and Schaffrath C., 1991, *Nonlinear time sequence analysis*, International Journal of Bifurcation and Chaos, **1**, 521–547.

Gray S., 1996, *Modeling the conditional distribution of interest rates as a regime-switch process*, Journal of Financial Economics, **42**, 27–62.

Guesnerie R. and Woodford M., 1992, *Endogenous fluctuations*, in J-J. Laffont (ed.), Advances in economic theory, Sixth World Congress. Cambridge University Press., 289–412.

Guillaume D. M., Pictet O. V., Müller U. A., and Dacorogna M. M., 1996, *Unveiling nonlinearities through time scale transformations*, unpublished manuscript, Financial Markets Group, London School of Economics.

Hamilton J., 1988, *Rational-expectations econometric analysis of changes in regime: an investigation of the term structure of interest rates*, Journal of Economics Dynamics and Control, 385–423.

Haubrich J. G. and Lo A. W., 1992, *The sources and nature of long-term dependence in the business cycle*, unpublished manuscript, Department of Finance, M.I.T.

Hinich M., 1982, *Testing for gaussianity and linearity of a stationary time series*, Journal of Time Series Analysis, **3**, 169–176.

Hsieh D., 1989, *Testing for non-linear dependence in daily foreign exchange rates*, Journal of business, **62**, 339–368.

Hsieh D. A., 1988, *The statistical properties of daily foreign exchange rates: 1974-1983*, Journal of International Economics, **24**, 129–145.

Hsieh D. A., 1991, *Chaos and nonlinear dynamics: Application to financial markets*, Journal of Finance, **46**, 1839–1877.

Hsieh D. A., 1992, *A nonlinear stochastic rational expectations model of exchange rates*, Journal of International Money and Finance, **11**, 235–250.

Hsieh D. A. and Kleidon W., 1996, *Asymmetric information in the foreign exchange markets*, in Pagano (eds) "The microstructure of the Foreign Exchange Markets", N.B.E.R.

International Monetary Fund ., 1993, *International capital markets. Part I. exchange rate management and international capital flows*, World Economic and Financial Surveys, **Washington, April 1993**, 1–79.

J. De Long B. e. a., 1990, *Noise trader risk in financial markets*, Journal of Political Economy, 703–738.

Jaditz T. and Sayers C., 1993, *Is chaos generic in economic data?*, International Journal of Bifurcation and Chaos, **3**, 745–755.

Jones C. M., Kaul G., and Lipson M. L., 1991, *Transactions, volumes and volatility*, mimeo, University of Michigan, School of Business Administration.

J.P.Morgan, 1994, *World Holiday and Time Guide*.

Kaplan J. and Yorke J., 1979, *Chaotic behavior of multi-dimensional difference equations*, in H. Peitgen and H. Walther (eds), Functional differential equations and approximation of fixed points, Lectures notes in Mathematics, Springer-Verlag, **730**, 204–227.

Kareken J. and Wallace N., 1981, *On the indeterminacy of equilibrium exchange rates*, Quaterly Journal of Economics, 202–222.

Lamoureux C. G. and Lastrapes W. D., 1990, *Heteroskedasticity in stock return data: Volume versus GARCH effects*, The Journal of Finance, **45**(1), 221–229.

LeBaron B., 1996, *Technical trading rule profitability and foreign exchange intervention*, NBER Working Paper, **5545**.

Lee T.-H., White H., and Granger C. W. J., 1993, *Testing for neglected nonlinearity in time series models*, Journal of Econometrics, **56**, 269–290.

Levich R., 1985, *Empirical studies of exchange rates: price behavior, rate determination and market efficiency*, in R. Jones and P. Kenen (eds.), "Handbook of International Economics", **2**, 979–1040.

Levich R. M. and Thomas L. R. III., 1993, *The significance of technical trading-rule profits in the foreign exchange market: a bootstrap approach*, Journal of International Money and Finance, **12**(5), 451–474.

Li T. and Yorke J., 1975, *Period three implies chaos*, American Mathematical Monthly, **82**, 985–992.

Lo A. W. and MacKinlay A. C., 1988, *Stock market prices do not follow random walks: evidence from a simple specification test*, The Review of Financial Studies, **1**, 41–66.

Loretan M. and Phillips P. C. B., 1994, *Testing the covariance stationarity of heavy-tailed time series*, Journal of Empirical Finance, **1**(2), 211–248.

Lucas R., 1976, *Econometric policy evaluation: a critique*, Carnegie-Rochester Series on Public Policy, **1**, 19–46.

Lyons R., 1999, *The Microstructure Approach to Exchanges Rates*, MIT Press.

Lyons R. K., 1995, *Test of microstructural hypotheses in the foreign exchange market*, Journal of Financial Economics, 321–351.

Lyons R. K., 1996a, *Foreign exchange volume: sound and fury signifying nothing?*, in J. Frankel et al. (eds.), The Microstructure of Foreign Exchange Markets, University of Chicago, 183–201.

Lyons R. K., 1996b, *Optimal transparency in a dealership market with an application to foreign exchange*, Journal of Financial Intermediation, 225–254.

Lyons R. K., 1997, *A simultaneous trade model of the foreign exchange hot potato*, Journal of International Economics, **42**, 275–298.

Madhavan A. and Smith S., 1991, *A bayesian model of intra-day specialist trading*, Journal of Financial Economics, **30**, 99–134.

Mandelbrot B. B., 1963, *The variation of certain speculative prices*, Journal of Business, **36**, 394–419.

Mandelbrot B. B., 1983, *The Fractal Geometry of Nature*, W.H.Freeman and Company, New York.

Mandelbrot B. B. and Taylor H. M., 1967, *On the distribution of stock prices differences*, Operations Research, **15**, 1057–1062.

Mark N., 1995, *Exchange rates and fundamentals: Evidence on long-horizon predictability*, American Economic Review, **85**(1), 201–218.

Mayfield E. and Mizrach B., 1992, *On determining the dimension of real-time stock-price data*, Journal of Business and Economic Statistics, **10**, 367–374.

McCulloch J. H., 1994, *Measuring tail thickness in order to estimate the stable index α: a critique*, Mimeo, Ohio State University, 1–34.

McFarland J. W., Petit R. R., and Sung S. K., 1982, *The distribution of foreign exchange price changes: trading day effects and risk measurement*, The Journal of Finance, **37**(3), 693–715.

Meese R. A. and Rogoff J., 1983, *Empirical exchange rate models of the seventies, do they fit out of sample ?*, Journal of International Economics, **14**, 3–24.

Meyers T. A., 1989, *Technical Analysis Course*, Probus Publishing Company, Chicago, Illinois.

Mirowski P., 1990, *From mandelbrot to chaos in economic theory*, Southern Economic Journal, **57**, 289–307.

Müller U. A., 1992, *Design of a new intrinsic time τ and its use in the Unbiased Forecaster (UBF)*, Internal document UAM.1992-05-18, Olsen & Associates, Seefeldstrasse 233, 8008 Zürich, Switzerland.

Müller U. A., 1993, *Statistics of variables observed over overlapping intervals*, Internal document UAM.1993-06-18, Olsen & Associates, Seefeldstrasse 233, 8008 Zürich, Switzerland.

Müller U. A., Dacorogna M. M., Davé R. D., Olsen R. B., Pictet O. V., and von Weizsäcker J. E., 1997, *Volatilities and trends of different time resolutions - analyzing the dynamics of market components*, forthcoming in Journal of Empirical Finance.

Müller U. A., Dacorogna M. M., Davé R. D., Pictet O. V., Olsen R. B., and Ward J. R., 1993, *Fractals and intrinsic time - a challenge to econometricians*, Invited presentation at the XXXIXth International AEA Conference on Real Time Econometrics, 14-15 Oct 1993 in Luxembourg, and the 4th International PASE Workshop, 22-26 Nov 1993 in Ascona (Switzerland); also in "Erfolgreiche Zinsprognose", ed. by B. Lüthje, Verband öffentlicher Banken, Bonn 1994, ISBN 3-927466-20-4; UAM.1993-08-16, Olsen & Associates, Seefeldstrasse 233, 8008 Zürich, Switzerland.

Müller U. A., Dacorogna M. M., Olsen R. B., Pictet O. V., Schwarz M., and Morgenegg C., 1990, *Statistical study of foreign exchange rates, empirical evidence of a price change scaling law, and intraday analysis*, Journal of Banking and Finance, **14**, 1189–1208.

Müller U. A. and Sgier R. G., 1992, *Statistical analysis of intraday bid-ask spreads in the foreign exchange market*, Internal document UAM.1992-04-10, Olsen & Associates, Seefeldstrasse 233, 8008 Zürich, Switzerland.

Mussa M., 1979, *Empirical regularities in the behavior of exchange rates and theories of the foreign exchange market*, Carnegie-Rochester Series on Public Policy, 9–57.

Nelson D., 1990, *Arch models as diffusion approximations*, Journal of Econometrics, **45**, 7–39.

Nerenberg M. and Essex C., 1990, *Correlation dimension and systematic geometric effects*, Physical Review A, **42**, 7065–7074.

Obstfeld M. and Stockman A., 1985, *Exchange rate dynamics*, in R. Jones and P. Kenen (eds.), Handbook of International Economics, **2**, 917–977.

O'Haara M., 1995, *Market Microstructure Theory*, Blackwell, Cambridge, Massachussets.

Packard N., Crutchfield P., Farmer D., and Shaw S., 1980, *Geometry from a time series*, Physical Review Letters, **45**, 712–716.

Peiers B., 1997, *Informed traders, intervention, and price leadership: A deeper viez of the microstructure of the foreign exchange market*, Journal of Finance, **52**, 1589–1614.

Peters E. E., 1989, *Fractal structure in the capital markets*, Financial Analysts Journal, **1989**(July/August), 32–37.

Petersen M. A. and Fialkowski D., 1994, *Posted versus effective spreads, good prices or bad quotes?*, Journal of Financial Economics, **35**(3), 269–292.

Poterba J. M. and Summers L. H., 1988, *Mean reversion in stock prices: evidence and implications*, Journal of Financial Economics, **22**, 27–59.

R. C. and Goodhart C., 1993, *Chartism: a controlled experiment*, Journal of International Securities Markets, **7**, 173–186.

Ramsey J. and Rothman P., 1992, *A reassesment of dimension calculations using some monetary data*, Technical Report 92-28, C.V. Starr Center for Applied Economics, N-Y University, 1–1.

Ramsey J. B., Sayers C. L., and Rothman P., 1990, *The statistical properties of dimension calculations using small data sets: some economic applications*, International Economic Review, **31**, 991–1020.

Ramsey J. B. and Yuan H.-J., 1989, *Bias and error bars in dimension calculations and their evaluation in some simple models*, Physics Letters A, **134**, 287–297.

Roy A. D., 1952, *Safety first the holding of assets*, Econometrica, **20**, 431–449.

Ruelle D., 1989, *Chaotic evolution and strange attractors*, Cambridge University Press.

Sauer T., Yorke J., and Casdagli M., 1991, *Embedology*, Journal of Statistical Physics, **65**, 311–337.

Scheinkman J. and LeBaron B., 1989, *Nonlinear dynamics and stock returns*, Journal of Business, **62**, 311–337.

Schreiber T., 1993, *Extremely simple nonlinear noise-reduction method*, Physical Review E, **47**, 2401–2404.

Schreiber T. and Grassberger P., 1991, *A simple noise-reduction method*, Physical Letters A, **160**, 411–422.

Smith L., 1988, *Intrinsic limits on dimension calculations*, Physical Letters A, **133**, 283–288.

Stock J. H., 1988, *Estimating continuous-time processes subject to time deformation*, Journal of the American Statistical Association, **83**(401), 77–85.

Subrahmanyam A., 1991, *Risk aversion, market liquidity, and price efficiency*, The Review of Financial Studies, **4**, 417–441.

Surajaras P. and Sweeney R., 1992, *Profit-making speculation in foreign exchange markets*, Westview Press.

Suvanto A., 1993, *Foreign exchange dealing*, ETLA, the Research Institute of the Finnish Economy, 1–132.

Svensson L. E., 1992, *An interpretation of recent research on exchange rate target zones*, Journal of Economic Perspectives, **6**(4), 119–144.

Takagi S., 1991, *Exchange rate expectations. a survey of survey studies.*, IMF Staff Papers., **38**, 156–183.

Takens F., 1981, *Detecting strange attractors in turbulence*, in D. Rand and L. Young (eds), Dynamical systems and turbulence, Lecture Notes in Mathematics, Springer-Verlag, **898**, 366–381.

Tata F. and Vassilicos C., 1991, *Is there chaos in economic time series? a study of the stock and the foreign exchange markets*, London School of Economics discussion papers, **120**.

Tauchen G. E. and Pitts M., 1983, *The price variability-volume relationship on speculative markets*, Econometrica, **51**, 485–505.

Taylor M. P. and Allen H., 1992, *The use of technical analysis in the foreign exchange market*, Journal of International Money and Finance, **11**, 304–314.

Taylor S. J., 1988, *Modelling Financial Time Series*, J. Wiley & Sons, Chichester.

Theiler J., 1986, *Spurious dimension from correlation algorithms applied to limited time-series data*, Physical Review A, **34**, 2427–2432.

Vassilicos J., 1990, *Are financial markets chaotic? a preliminary study of the foreign exchange market*, London School of Economics Financial Markets Group discussion paper, **86**.

Wasserfallen W. and Zimmermann H., 1985, *The behavior of intra-daily exchange rates*, Journal of Banking and Finance, **9**, 55–72.

Weber A., 1995, *Exchange rates and the effectiveness of central bank intervention: New evidence for the g-3 and the ems*, Unpublished manuscript, University of Bonn, 1–23.

Westerfield J., 1977, *Empirical properties of foreign exchange rates under fixed and floating rate regimes*, Journal of International Economics, 181–200.

White H., 1980, *A heteroscedasticity-consistent covariance matrix and a direct test for heteroscedasticity*, Econometrica, **48**(4), 421–448.

Zhou B., 1993, *Forecasting foreign exchange rates subject to devolatilization*, Working Paper. MIT Sloan School, **3510**, 1–24.

Index

161